ACROSS THE CHANNEL

Major-General Sir Donald Banks KCB DSO MC TD (1891-1975)

ACROSS THE CHANNEL

The Memoirs of
Major-General
Sir Donald Banks
KCB DSO MC TD

Foreword by
Sir Richard Collas, Bailiff of Guernsey

Introduction by Stephen Foote

Blue Ormer
2020

Published by Blue Ormer Publishing, 2020.
www.blueormer.co.uk

Main text © The Estate of Sir Donald Banks.
Edited by Dawn Smith (née Banks).

Foreword © Sir Richard Collas.
Introduction © Stephen Foote.

Cover illustration © Melanie Dodd (née Banks).
All illustrations, unless otherwise credited, are from the Banks family collection.

ISBN 978-1-9993415-1-0

Printed by Short Run Press, Exeter.

CONTENTS

FOREWORD

I warmly welcome this publication of the memoirs of an extraordinary man who, until now, has not been properly recognised in the island of his birth. This book will raise awareness and preserve for future generations the remarkable achievements of a Guernseyman whose service to King and country in two world wars and in peacetime is quite remarkable.

Like many islanders leaving school, Donald Banks left his home island and moved to London to make a life for himself. In his wildest dreams, he could not have imagined the opportunities that would present themselves. The Latin proverb that translates as '*fortune favours the brave*' springs to mind as there were a number of occasions throughout his life when it could be said that Sir Donald was in the right place at the right time.

However, that would not do justice to the many inherent qualities he brought to everything he did. In wartime he was a brave soldier whose leadership skills earned the respect not only of the men who served with him but of his superiors who entrusted him with ever increasing responsibilities. Yet he was a modest man who makes little mention of the honours conferred on him: a Military Cross, the Distinguished Service Order, *Croix de Guerre,* US Legion of Merit and two mentions in dispatches. His matter of fact description of the fighting in the trenches in close combat with the enemy are told with light hearted anecdotes revealing a sense of humour along with a surprising degree of compassion. His description of the booby-traps left behind by the retreating enemy as 'unworthy of good soldiers' reveals a sense of fair play and decency even at times of greatest threat.

Sir Donald's rise through the ranks of the General Post Office to the position of its first Director General and his subsequent senior posts at the Air Ministry and the Department of Petroleum Warfare are told with a fascinating description of the innovation and enterprise of those he led and commanded but reveal less of the character of the man himself.

There are many mentions of his love of Guernsey and of happy memories of his childhood on the island but sadly he does not describe his contribution to the welfare of evacuated islanders in the Second World War and the founding of the Guernsey Society nor the contribution he made to the plans for the reconstitution and rehabilitation of the Channel Islands after their Liberation. Those events will be commemorated with the unveiling of a blue plaque in St Peter Port High Street as part of the commemorations of the 75th anniversary of the Liberation.

I congratulate Sir Donald's daughters and Stephen Foote for their hard work in publishing this work and for the interesting footnotes they have added to the original text. I commend the book to all who take pride in the achievements of our fellow islanders whose hard work and enterprise beyond our shores have ensured a better and safer world for us all to enjoy.

Sir Richard Collas
Bailiff of Guernsey
Royal Court
January 2020

INTRODUCTION

On 12 July 1975, the *Daily Telegraph* carried the obituary of Sir Donald Banks, which declared him to be:

> ... a man of ideas whose versatility contributed much to the national well-being in war and peace.

And yet in 2019, when the planning application to erect a blue plaque on his childhood home in St Peter Port was published in the local newspaper, BBC Radio Guernsey sent out an appeal for information on this apparently-forgotten Guernseyman.

There can be few individuals who have been at the centre of so many momentous events of the 20th century: the Battle of the Somme, the chartering of the BBC, the increase of women in the workplace during the 1920s, the rearmament of the air force in the build-up to World War 2, the evacuation of Dunkirk, the Battle of Britain, the preparations for D-Day and the liberation of Europe.

At the General Post Office, together with Postmaster General, Sir Kingsley Wood, Sir Donald Banks started to transform the GPO from a Victorian public service into a more business-like twentieth-century organisation. At the time, the GPO was responsible for the Royal Mail, its post offices, the BBC, the Post Office Savings Bank and the national telephone service. The services introduced during this period included: off-peak call rates, the speaking clock, the emergency services ('999'), the Empire Air Mail Scheme (forerunner of air mail), the Greetings Telegramme and the national rollout of Sir Giles Gilbert Scott's iconic red telephone kiosk design.

Publishing these memoirs is intended to help raise awareness of the life and achievements of this distinguished soldier, civil servant and devoted Guernseyman.

Thomas Macdonald Banks was born in St Peter Port, Guernsey on 31 March 1891. His father, Thomas Brownsort Banks, had bought a bookshop at 43 High Street when he moved to the island from Wolverhampton in the previous decade. Thomas senior was the son of a wine and spirit merchant in that city, and his grandfather established Banks' Brewery (which retains its own identity as part of Marston's Brewery to this day). His mother, Margaret (née Roebuck), was the daughter of a bookshop owner and granddaughter of a Scottish congregationalist minister. In the opening paragraph of his memoir, he confesses to having no idea why his parents moved to Guernsey. It seems likely that, by entering the book trade, his father was looking to overcome any concerns his puritanical in-laws had about their daughter marrying into a family whose wealth was derived from alcohol. Thomas senior returned to Wolverhampton in 1889 where he and Margaret were married in Queen Street Congregational Chapel; their eldest daughter Blanche was born in Guernsey the year after. Thomas Macdonald followed in 1891 and Maurice in 1898. Thomas Macdonald was shortened to Donald – a name which remained with him throughout his life.

Carefree summer at Saints Bay
(left to right: Blanche, unknown, Donald, Maurice)

T B Banks' bookshop prospered – providing books as prizes for the annual Elizabeth College prize-giving ceremony as well as selling stationery, a lending library, publishing his own books and producing postcards, guides and maps for the growing tourist market. When it became clear that none of his children was interested in continuing the family business, he took on a junior partner, Frank Brownsey, from Bristol. Together they expanded the business further, setting up a printing business at Le Tourgand in the Pollet. Banks senior owned one of the first motor cars in the island, and during the summers, the family used to rent an old granite Napoleonic defence tower at Saints Bay as a summer house. Although it was just two miles south of St Peter Port, it was nestled into the cliffs just above this picturesque bay on the island's south coast. The family have photographs, journals and poetry composed at the tower during these summer breaks, recording happy family memories of carefree summers in the early years of the 20th century before World War 1.

Donald and Maurice attended Elizabeth College, the local public school. Donald was a successful scholar, managing to secure at least one award each year at the annual prize-giving service. In 1909 – his final year – he won a total of seven! One book was given to the most promising student in each subject. Donald also joined the Officer Training Corps and was on the shooting team. He made many lasting friends at school – which was to stand him in good stead later in his life.

These memoirs follow his career from joining the British Civil Service in 1909 through to the end of World War 2. *Across the Channel* is not the first book Sir Donald Banks wrote. His first, *With the 10th Essex in France*, is the battalion's official history, cowritten with Captain Randolph Chell. It recounts the battalion's WW1 experience, in a *Boy's Own* style typical of many regimental histories of the period. In a rather impersonal way, it recalls many of the battles in which the battalion was engaged, with a particular focus on the battles fought and medals won. However, it includes few details of any of his own escapades. His account here is far more vivid and personal: from the hilarious account of how he managed to circumvent army bureaucracy to transfer from the regular army to one of Kitchener's Army battalions – through to his eyewitness account of the Battle of the Somme. By the end of the war, he had been awarded the Military Cross, Distinguished Service Order and *Croix de Guerre*, and had graduated from a Private in the London Yeomanry to Lieutenant-Colonel, the commanding officer of his own battalion.

After World War 2, he published *Flame Over Britain* about his experiences as Director General of the Petroleum Warfare Department (PWD). Their relentless pursuit of innovative applications for the country's excess fuel supplies resulted in FIDO (fog dispersal at airfields), PLUTO (to ensure continuity of fuel supplies to Europe's liberating army after D-Day) as well as the adaptation of flamethrowers onto the US Army's tanks – for which he was awarded the Legion of Merit by President Truman. Although this was technically a civil service role, he was promoted to the rank of Major-General to reflect the number of military units under his command.

Across the Channel was intended to be his third book and was written during his retirement. Although undated, there are several clues in the text. Chapter 2 refers to 1963 as the current year whilst the references to England's 1966 World Cup victory, Harold Wilson's battles with the trade unions and the plans to restructure the Post Office in 1967 suggest it was written over a longer period of time. Although it was never published, the manuscript has remained in the possession of the family ever since. The original handwritten manuscript was deposited in the Imperial War Museum and can be found amongst the Sir Donald Banks collection.

Whilst this memoir contains details of Sir Donald Banks' long and varied career not found elsewhere – it is interesting to note what he chose to leave out.

His modesty evidently resulted in only passing references to the circumstances which led to his World War 1 gallantry medals. Detailed citations for these awards have therefore been added as footnotes to the relevant passages. A further example of his courage is the letter he wrote to his mother on the eve of the Battle of the Somme.[1]

At the Air Ministry in 1936, there was controversy surrounding the departure of his predecessor, Sir Christopher Bullock, who had been dismissed for misconduct. The two men had worked together on the Empire Air Mail Scheme the year before and would have known each other well. It would have been interesting to hear Sir Donald's perspectives on the circumstances of Bullock's departure.

Over three years later, when he was transferred to the Import Duties Advisory Committee during one of the most critical periods of the Air Ministry's history, questions were asked in the House of Commons as to why he was leaving (having 'rendered valuable services to civil aviation'). In this account he cryptically talks of a 'palace revolution' while he was in Australasia, but there are few details of his role in turning around the production of fighter aircraft.[2] It is clear that, once reunited with Sir Kingsley Wood, with whom he had successfully transformed the Post Office, they managed to scale up the production of modern fighters from 80 per month in March 1938 to 1,000 per month by early 1939. Without this turnaround the RAF would have been ill-prepared for the Battle of Britain.

Several of the later chapters relate the contribution of the Petroleum Warfare Department to the war effort under his command. However, there are no details of his receiving the Legion of Merit in 1946. Nor are there any details of his dispute with the Treasury over the publication the same year of *Flame Over Britain* which resulted in several passages being removed or toned down.[3]

Apart from the first chapter, there is little here about his lifelong association with his native Guernsey. Although he never returned to live there after he moved to London in 1909, he retained a strong and loyal association with the island and its

1   See Appendix I.
2   See Appendix III for the article which appeared in *Time Magazine*, 19 May 1939 which sheds more light on this episode.
3   *Publication of Flame Over Britain*, T273/230, National Archives, Kew.

people throughout his life. Particularly during World War 2, when the Channel Islands were occupied by German forces, he spent a considerable amount of effort using his Whitehall connections to ensure the plight of the islanders was not overlooked. Both he and Dorothy were actively involved with the Channel Islands Refugee Committee based at Upper Brooke Street in London. He became a Director of Elizabeth College, his *alma mater* and, together with several fellow alumni, strove to ensure that the college could continue to exist in exile in Derbyshire. In 1942, he broadcast a message of reassurance to islanders on national radio at the invitation of the BBC.[4] In 1943, he founded the Guernsey Society and built a membership of over 400 influential exiled and expatriate islanders from all walks of life. This enabled him to make authoritative representations to the Home Office on the island's behalf. He chaired a symposium in Oxford that summer, with representatives from all of the Channel Islands which led to the publication of *Nos Iles* in 1944: a blueprint for the liberation of the islands and the reconstruction of their economies after the war. It appears to have galvanised the Home Office into planning for the liberation of the islands, as there is no evidence of such efforts before the start of his campaign.

On Sir Donald's retirement from the civil service in 1947, Sir Bernard Westall – chairman of De La Rue and former officer of the 10th Essex Regiment – invited his former commanding officer to join the Board of Directors. Having the former Director General of the British Post Office as a Director was a valuable asset in developing international business opportunities for their postage stamps and bank note business with other countries around the world. De La Rue was founded by Guernseyman Thomas De La Rue in 1821. When the Banks family decided to sell their father's business in Guernsey – which had continued operating throughout the German occupation – Sir Donald persuaded De La Rue to acquire it, re-establishing the link between the company and its founder's birthplace almost a century after its foundation. The printing business at

---

4   The full text of this speech 'Sand and Granite' is reproduced in Appendix IV.

Le Tourgand in St Peter Port was acquired by De La Rue in 1947. When they eventually closed the business in 1963, the building was converted into a public house, which is still known as the Thomas De La Rue today.

Last but not least, there are few references to his family life. Donald married Dorothy Webster in 1921, and they had one daughter, Dawn (who is mentioned in Chapter 11). Dorothy's father, Dr Norman Webster, was a prominent homeopathic doctor from Worcestershire, who practiced from his home *Roseneath* in St Peter Port. Her mother, Annie Elizabeth (neé Simpson) was from Yorkshire.

In 1947, Dorothy died of cancer. The following year he remarried, to Elizabeth Bradley, with Sir Bernard Westall as his best man. Sir Donald and Elizabeth had two children – Peter and Melanie. They purchased Cadnam Lodge in the New Forest, where he kept a herd of Guernsey cattle.

There is a family story that, on his retirement, Sir Donald was offered the position of Lieutenant-Governor of Guernsey – which he declined for personal reasons. If he had accepted, he would have become the first Guernsey-born Lieutenant-Governor in 600 years – an honour that was eventually achieved by Sir Peter Le Cheminant in 1980.

In evaluating how Sir Donald succeeded in such diverse areas as the army, the General Post Office and the Petroleum Warfare Department, the common denominator is his leadership skills. David Godfrey, former Vice President of the Guernsey Society who remembered the society's founder well, summed it up: 'Sir Donald Banks was a man of action – when he got involved in something, things really started to happen'. It is ironic that, despite joining the civil service in 1909, it was the army that recognised and developed his leadership potential during World War 1 – it only came to the attention of the civil service when he returned from the war with so many decorations.[5]

He was a keen student of the emerging fields of management

5   See Appendix II for the testimony of one of the men who served under him in both.

science and organisational theory. Much of this work was pioneered by Lyndall Urwick, with whom he worked at the Post Office and later in the PWD. Sir Donald recognised that innovation required not only skilled scientists and engineers to develop new ideas, but also an organisational culture in which these ideas could flourish. He understood how the civil service worked and was keenly aware of its shortcomings. From the outset, he ensured that the PWD had a level of financial independence from the traditional civil service controls which constrain innovative thinking, discourage risk-taking and create barriers to inter-departmental cooperation.

> How important it was transpired only in the course of later developments, for our financial independence enabled us to go ahead with experiments and to pursue ideas with a flexibility that would have been difficult to obtain under the *ægis* of larger organisations.[6]

He also built collaborative links with industry and the various branches of the armed services necessary to implement these developments. The results speak for themselves: in the space of a few years, the PWD developed and delivered new applications for the use of petroleum, firstly in the defence of Britain (FIDO, flame barrage) and then, as the war progressed, in the liberation of Europe (PLUTO, flamethrowers on tanks).

After the war, the achievements of the Petroleum Warfare Department were widely praised. Winston Churchill declared: 'Operation Pluto was a remarkable feat of British engineering, distinguished by its originality, pursued with tenacity and crowned by complete success' and General Eisenhower considered its contribution to the success of D-Day 'second in daring only to the artificial Mulberry harbors' .

In 2013, when the Guernsey Society was considering ways in which to celebrate its 70th Anniversary, I suggested we campaign

---

6   *Flame Over Britain*, p.29

for a blue plaque to be erected on the childhood home of our founder.

The application was accepted by the island's Blue Plaques Committee, but sadly rejected by the tenants of the building at the time. Five years later, when we learned that the shop's tenants had moved out, we contacted the committee suggesting they approach the new tenants. Fortunately they were more receptive to the idea, and the campaign was back on track, leading to the unveiling of the plaque on the eve of the 75th Anniversary of Liberation Day on 8 May 2020.

It's a fitting tribute to a devoted Guernseyman.

Stephen Foote
Guernsey, December 2019

ACKNOWLEDGEMENTS

I would like to thank Dawn Smith and Melanie Dodd, Sir Donald's daughters, and their families for their support and encouragement. In particular Dawn's tireless efforts to complete a final edit of her father's work and prepare it for publication, and Melanie's illustration for the front cover of this book.

I would also like to thank: the Imperial War Museum, National Portrait Gallery and Royal Mail Archive for permission to reproduce images from their collections; Keith Le Page, present chairman, and the Council of the Guernsey Society, for supporting the blue plaque campaign; Helen Glencross, acting Head of Guernsey Heritage Services, for her support; Stephen Smith and Colin Vaudin for advice on military matters; Jane Mosse and Mary Carey for proof reading and Sir Richard Collas, Bailiff of Guernsey, for unveiling the plaque and agreeing to write the Foreword to this book.

T B Banks bookshop, 43 High Street, St Peter Port
(T B Banks standing in doorway,
a young Donald setting out to deliver newspapers)

1

GUERNSEY PRELUDE

It is not recorded what led my parents, in the year of the first Victorian Jubilee, to migrate from Staffordshire to the Channel Islands. But my grandfather lent my father sufficient to buy a promising bookshop in the Grande Rue, St Peter Port, Guernsey; by the time the business there was established (and the loan repaid with suitable interest), Queen Victoria had notched up her Diamond Anniversary and I was old enough to register in my first memories the celebrations which marked the Jubilee of 1897.

The old square-rigged and the new iron-clad ships of the much vaunted British Navy anchored in the roadstead off the island and occupied completely the narrow straits of the Little Russell between Guernsey and Herm and Jethou (much as in later days and circumstances the vast Invasion Armada filled the Solent in front of our house at Lymington before D-Day in 1944).

A long winding cavalcade paraded the Town from the remoter parts of Guernsey and consisted of representations of the many ancient features of island history – its conscripted army of artillery, engineers and three battalions of infantry, drafted from a public lottery held in the Market Place to the immense interest of the populace. One float depicted the immemorial custom of the *Clameur de Haro*[1] handed down from the days when the island was a fief of the Duchy of Normandy; another the conflicts of Cromwellian days when Castle Cornet held out for nine years against the bombardments of the Parliamentarians; still another recalled the recent controversies of sterling versus French currency, featured in the display in which we children played a part.

For long enough both English and French silver were in common circulation. But sterling was worth more in those solid

---

1   An ancient legal injunction for settling disputes over land. It is based on Norman law and still legally enforceable in the Channel Islands.

Elizabeth College Officer Training Corps, c 1908
(Sgt Banks seated centre)

days. So, wherever we could, children used to collect shillings and half-crowns which were worth a penny more in the shilling than the French money. Armed with a pocketful of sterling one could go to the local sweet shops and buy sixpenny worth of Guernsey 'sugars' by handing in six shillings worth of sterling and receiving six shillings back. It was an idyllic lesson in foreign exchange, but not necessarily for the shopkeeper. So an agitation for sterling only was being staged by the commercial elements. A tableau on a float was surmounted by a magnificent busty figure of Britannia with a lion couchant at her feet. On either side marched a file of soldiery, one side in the spiked helmets of the British uniform and the other in the *képis* of the French. Every now and then one side would menace the other, whereupon Britannia would intervene with her trident pointing to the £ signs on which she was enthroned, the gentleman in the lion's skin would wave his paws and roar violently and peace would be restored – a miniature display of the Pax Britannica which we were celebrating at the end of that notable nineteenth century.

The twentieth century saw the abolition of the Militia and of compulsory military service handed down from the time of the Conquest and inapplicable elsewhere in the Empire. So vanished the glory of the parade of the Island-in-Arms in honour of the Queen's Birthday on the Belvedere of Fort George overlooking the deep blue of the archipelago of the smaller islands. Six or seven thousand soldiers in scarlet and blue were there with the blare of half a dozen military bands, while the rest of the island population packed every vantage-point in their Sunday finery.

The patriotic fervour was immense. School children used to chant for days in advance:-

> The Twenty-fourth of May
> Is the Queen's Birthday.
> If you don't give us a holiday
> We'll all run away!

After a celebratory *feu de joie* (with blank ammunition) involving the whole parade (in which many year-long grudges were paid off by undetected aiming from the rear ranks), the moment arrived when the Royal Standard was hoisted. The national anthem was played by the massed bands (variously tuned) amid the thunder of the guns of Castle Cornet and of the Navy in the roadstead. The enthusiasm was indescribable.

The Militia succumbed eventually to the economy axe which inevitably swings between inevitable wars. But before its disappearance there occurred the unique incident in which the whole of the North Regiment, having mutinied on parade under an unpopular adjutant, was sentenced by the Royal Court to spend a week in gaol.

The local prison was not normally required to accommodate more than a small peak-load of Saturday-night drunks who used to be hurried there on a tradesman's handcart, conveniently parked for the purpose outside the Constables' Office. So a shift system was devised whereby a certain number of militiamen

T B Banks Bookshop, 43 High Street

were detailed to parade at the Court each Monday morning and were released on Saturday morning (thus neatly providing for the overnight Saturday drunks). The soldiers were marched into the inner recesses of the gaol and there relieved of their rifles and helmets. These were restored to them at the end of the week so that they could emerge in the triumph of full military regalia to greet their assembled relatives and friends at the end of the week.

The total police force at that time was six, under the command of a redoubtable Sergeant Burley, who ruled us all in the island with a paternal benevolence. So it was obvious that some mutual do-it-yourself arrangement was desirable. It suited the authorities, who took care to provide good fare in gaol; it suited the rebellious northerners admirably too, as times happened to be bad in the granite industry and a week's free board and lodging at the expense of the British Exchequer (with a glorious binge-up upon release) was not to be despised.

*Blanche, Donald and Maurice Banks pictured on
top of the loophole tower at Saints Bay in Guernsey
where the family used to spend their summers.*

2
ACROSS THE CHANNEL

The total area of Guernsey is twenty-five square miles with a phenomenal population density of about a thousand to the square mile. Combined with the other islands in the Bailiwick (Sark, Brecqhou, Herm, Jethou, Alderney and Lihou) this formed a completely self-governing entity, entirely separate from Jersey. However there were obvious limitations to providing careers for her sons. Indeed, over the centuries, right back to the organising of the expeditionary force for the conquest of England by Duke William of Normandy, it had been traditional for the rising generations to choose between service 'overseas' and home-based activities.

So, when I was nearing the end of my schooling at Elizabeth College, there was great debate in my family as to whether I should try to become a large-sized conger in the local waters or cross the Channel to the greater islands beyond.

By custom, most of the government appointments connected with the Royal Court were the appanage of the old island families. I had participated in a minor capacity in some local enterprises in the making of bricks and in tomato-growing, where we succeeded in exporting up to forty tons a year. There was also the expanding prospect of my father's business, to which he had added a prospering printing side where I used to earn a bit of extra pocket-money by operating a platen machine.

On the other hand, I remember that the electrical and communications sector on the mainland – then very much of what later came to be called a 'growth industry' – attracted me at the time. But Fate was to steer me into that in later days by other approaches. Into these many considerations the Civil Service Commission suddenly injected an announcement of 'Intermediate' appointments in the Admiralty and other government offices. It was a new class designed to attract public school boys who could not afford the expensive University preparations necessary for a First Division entry. As I had just missed out on the classical subjects necessary to qualify for the Channel Islander scholarships which Charles II had instituted at Oxford in grateful recognition of the hospitality and support that the islands had given him in his exile, the new jobs came just at the right moment to settle my problems.

I remember one enthusiastic friend who painted a vivid picture of the excitement of being at the Admiralty when a future order was given to mobilise the Fleet. Alas! there were only three vacancies offered in the Admiralty and as I placed eighth in the examination, it was left to Winston Churchill to mobilise the Fleet and I was posted to the less exciting environment of the Exchequer and Audit Department.

It all sounded important enough, however. No issue of Government funds could be made without the certificate of the Comptroller and Auditor General; all expenditure by any of the departments of state was subject to his scrutiny; he was the national watchdog and woe betide any spending by profligate ministers who tried to evade his questioning. It was all glorious Gladstonian stuff reaching back indeed far before Gladstone to the days when the faithful Commons really did guard the public purse and control extortionate taxation on those they represented. But, like so many things in government life, it was very much *ex post facto*.

There was little indeed in the government machine to encourage active and practical looking-ahead. The rewards on the political side went mainly to ministers who played safe and dealt with the balls as they came down. Within the ministries this was reflected in the permanent staff attitude of scepticism to imaginative approaches and in a premium on stolid and pre-eminently safety-first administration. This, it can be argued, was all to the good as a mechanism of government, but there is a vague element running in our national nature of belief that some *deus ex machina* can be invoked in our rulers to guide us in our destinies. Government machinery, even under the stimulus of vigorous criticism, is a poor instrument for such a purpose – and particularly poor when enterprise is demanded.

In the case of the Exchequer and Audit Department the critical element, of course, was supreme. But even then, when it found the light of day in the strictures of the Comptroller and Auditor General and the proceedings of the Public Accounts Committee, the errors were revealed so long after the event and were so difficult to pin on the ministers responsible, that vast areas of potentially wasteful expenditure went uncontrolled at the time. Enormities like those that emerged in the aircraft contracts of later days had little more than a melancholy historical significance in the headlines.[1]

So the atmosphere in my first days of contact with the little Audit Office on the Victoria Embankment reflected nothing of the dynamism to which I had looked forward so glowingly in crossing the seas to the great world of London. The older Civil Service traditions lingered on and lent their own liveliness in the form of many extra-official activities. Being adjacent to Fleet Street made it feasible for one enterprising clerk to conduct the editorship of the *Poultry World* within the ambit of his office duties. Another, perhaps less heinously, was the drama critic for *The Times* along the street. A third managed to report the Balkan War for the *Daily Chronicle* in the course of his six weeks leave in Bulgaria. A particular friend of mine read for and passed his Bar examinations from the office and subsequently left the audit of the Irish accounts for the more immediate life of the Law Courts. This exploit led me to wonder whether I could surmount the First Division stockade which stood between me and the better opportunities of a Civil Service career, or at least escape from the eternal green pencil plod through the meticulously kept accounts of the Royal Irish Constabulary which had fallen to my lot.

The dividing line between the University entrants into the First Division of the Civil Service and the Second Division and other classes was very heavily drawn. It gave the highly qualified products of Oxford and Cambridge access to the leading positions in the Treasury, the Home Office and most of the Whitehall

---

1   A reference to the difficulties experienced by the Air Ministry in procuring fighters during the rearmament of the RAF before WW2.

departments; it also offered a choice of service in the Indian Civil Service, or a Cadetship, and often an eventual Governorship, in the Colonial Service. These indeed were glittering prizes which, like the ancient Mandarin system of China, were unconditioned by fortune or birth and offered unrestricted opportunities for the humblest. The main handicap was the very severe conditions of the competitive entrance examination, based as it was on the subjects for an honours degree at the older universities and extending for the duration of a month in the heat of the year in London. These were formidable obstacles when one was already in full-time employment, but there was a generous leave allowance in the job I was in: with strict economy in my holidays during the rest of the year this should cover the duration of the examination. The greatest difficulty lay in finding tuition in the evenings equal to the standards available to undergraduates at the Varsities with almost unlimited time at their disposal.

I ruefully counted over the eight golden sovereigns which came to me across the pay table at the end of each month, took stock of my exiguous past savings in the Post Office Savings Bank and of my likely wardrobe needs for the next few years. I would have to rely on my parents' help towards the expenses of getting home for holidays. It seemed that I could meet the comparatively light fees at the London School of Economics where Sidney Webb, reported to be on the examiners list of the Civil Service Commissioners, was lecturing in the Social Sciences. The Guildhall Library, with St Brides as an additional source for borrowing books, afforded opportunities for lunch-time study of set books and English Literature; although I remember incurring the displeasure of the librarian when the crumbs from my scanty luncheons of digestive biscuits were scattered amongst his precious wares. The greatest difficulties lay in securing tuition in Mathematics and Modern Languages. After a long search I discovered a dubious-looking cramming establishment on a top floor in Chancery Lane where the tutors seemed every whit as impecunious as I was. However, thanks to a little extra encouragement with a glass of cognac for my Italian tutor at the end of the evening session, I made some quite remarkable progress in the Italian tongue, unmatched, alas, by equal proficiency in the intricacies of Higher Mathematics.

For the rest of my expenses, I came to the conclusion that I must save on the fares from my lodgings in Muswell Hill by walking to and from King's Cross.[2] I ascribe a good many of my marks in languages to a pocket dictionary I carried and studied intermittently on the walk down the Gray's Inn Road and Fetter Lane, through the fascinating alleys of the Temple to the Victoria Embankment. Shoe leather worried me, but I sought to reduce the wear by lengthening my stride and by going up steps two at a time whenever feasible.

Those were the days of the growing German menace, of the spine-chilling play *The Englishman's Home*[3] and of the patriotic fervour for Dreadnoughts[4]: 'We want Eight/ And we won't wait.' Enthusiasm for military service pervaded the office.

I remember a stalwart sergeant in the Civil Service Rifles contending that the best way to clean a rifle was to discharge a live round through it; he promptly demonstrated this by firing one up the chimney in our small official room. The effect on the rifle may have been as claimed, but the noise was shattering and the soot almost buried us; such activities, together with the inclusion of kippers in our lunch-time preparations on the office fires, were sternly frowned upon by the department authorities.

Meanwhile, I was being subjected to some pressure by two cousins in the Royal Naval Volunteers and the London Yeomanry, respectively.[5] HMS *President*, which theoretically

---

2   Banks lodged in Wellfield Avenue, Muswell Hill with his uncle and aunt: Thomas Mitchelhill, a Scottish railway company manager, and Annie Mitchelhill (née Banks).

3   A play by Guy du Maurier that caused a sensation in London when it opened anonymously in 1909 under the title 'A Patriot'. Typical of the so-called 'invasion literature' popular just before WW1, it drew attention to Britain's lack of defences against attack and is credited with boosting recruitment in the Territorial Army.

4   The predominant class of battleship in the early 20th century. The prototype, named HMS *Dreadnought*, was launched in 1906.

5   Banks' cousin Oswald Kerfoot Davies served in the Royal Naval

housed all the officers of the Royal Navy serving with the Admiralty, as well as the several hundred weekend sailors who constituted the London Volunteer Reserve, was conveniently moored off the Embankment right opposite Audit House. So it was an easy matter to visit her, albeit somewhat perilous at some states of the tide in the absence of the gang-plank of more modern days. One found a very matey atmosphere aboard, but apart from what seemed to be eternal sessions of knotting and splicing there was comparatively little scope for a rollicking life on the ocean waves between Blackfriars and Waterloo Bridges.

The intensity of the activities of B Squadron of the London Sharpshooters Yeomanry was, however, a different matter altogether. They had their headquarters in a small house near Lords Cricket Ground, with a back garden connecting with the Royal Horse Artillery quarters at St Johns Wood. Over the mantelpiece in the Canteen a large notice proclaimed

THE HORSE IS A NOBLE ANIMAL. WE DON'T THINK.

It took a remarkably short time to test this assertion as one was given a quick shandy and hurried to a changing room and thence to the RHA Riding School, where the so-called nobility were assembled.

At that time BB Battery was then stationed there together with L Battery of later Néry fame (they won three V.C.s in one action). It was BB Battery to whom my fate was entrusted and who forthwith proceeded to teach me the hitherto unknown art of horseback riding by putting me over a series of low jumps with no more equipment than a numnah and a surcingle.[6] It was a revealing experience in many ways and to many parts of my anatomy.

The horses, I remember, all bore names beginning with B: Bolster, Bumper, Bronco and Bouncer; Blondie, Brunette,

---

Volunteer Reserve but it has not been possible to identify which of his cousins served in the London Yeomanry.

6   Without a saddle: the rider was mounted on the horse with nothing more than a blanket and saddle-girth to hold it in place.

Private TM Banks, London Yeomanry

Blossom, and Bébé; Boanerges, Bathsheba, Bugaboo and Boudicea.[7] Bolster, who was my first mount, looked mildly disapproving at the frequency with which her ample back was left unoccupied; but the limit was reached when I found that one was also expected to dismount and remount at the canter between the jumps.

The contrast between the comparative peacefulness of HMS *President* and the rip-roaring circus of the many Bs could not have been greater. But whether it was the sensation of activity or that of the full-dress green and gold Hussar uniform and the glossy black fur busby of the Sharpshooters, the Bs won hands down. We London Yeomen were an eye-catching lot in full finery, spurs and all, at the various evening functions in London or at weekends at Windsor or Aldershot or Canterbury on Bank Holidays. There were the purple, scarlet and gold Dragoons of Westminster, the sky-blue Lancer Roughriders of the City and the blue and gold Hussars of Middlesex. No wonder the more

---

7   Many years later, in the 1950s, DB similarly gave the cows in his Guernsey herd in Hampshire names beginning with with B (eg. Buttercup, Brandysnap and Boadicea).

sombrely-clad regiments of the Inns of Court, the Artists and the Westminster Rifles, would break into song when we appeared at their gatherings :-

Why were you born so beautiful?
Oh! Why were you born at all?

All these external occupations contrasted greatly with the routine of the Audit and the long slog of matitudinal and late-night superimposed studies, with an all too rapidly-approaching examination date of August, 1914. An outstanding, and perhaps ominous, memory of that period is the army manoeuvres of 1913 when the largest military force ever hitherto deployed in England conducted their exercises against the 'White' invaders through the plains of the Midlands. The London Mounted Brigade formed part of a complete Cavalry Division encamped one night in fields outside Towcester when the picketed horses of the Royal Scots Greys stampeded. The confusion as these grey wraiths galloped wildly in the darkness through the campfires and the serried lines of some thousands of tethered horses of the other units was unimaginable.

The first taste of military realism came my way in these exercises when as part of a screen of Sharpshooters' scouts on lonely reconnaissance in the Savernake Forest we detected the movement of large bodies of the 'White' forces attempting a dangerous outflanking movement. It was a profound experience for a two-man vedette[8] peering through the Wiltshire trees and then galloping hell-for-leather in the style of 'How they brought the news from Ghent' into a conclave of high-ranking officers assembled in a nearby village.

I reined up at the most important-looking General, saluted smartly and reported: 'Sir! Large body of the Enemy approaching from the immediate rear.' He glared at me fiercely: 'Enemy, Enemy! What the hell does it matter about the Enemy, boy? This is a General's conference.'

---

8   A sentry on horseback posted to watch the enemy's movements.

Perhaps many bloody encounters of the next four years were thus prophetically foreshadowed.

The climactic date for the First Division examination was August 4th, 1914 and I was preparing to leave my lodgings for Piccadilly when the postman pushed under the door a long official envelope ordering my immediate mobilisation. Here was catastrophe – universal and personal – on one short sheet!

I made an appeal in person to Sir Henry Gibson, the august Comptroller and Auditor General, whom I had never seen before; fortunately, he was intrigued by my unusual ambitions and proved to be the embodiment of sympathy. He secured an intervention by the War Office for me and exemption from immediate military duties for four weeks.

Those August days were those:

> ... when heaven was falling,
> The hour when earth's foundations fled.[9]

However, incarcerated for an endless succession of three-hour examination papers in the solidity of Burlington Gardens I don't know that I was particularly sensitive to these world-shaking events beyond a vague fretting that I should be too late to justify my yeoman's spurs and a firm and satisfying belief that the angelic hosts had intervened on our side at the Battle of Mons.[10]

How closely we in our off-shore island are identified with the fortunes of Europe at such times as these. An historical recital – Crécy and Agincourt, Dunkirk Roads and the Spanish Netherlands, Oudenarde and Malplaquet, Waterloo and Paris – shows that, through the centuries, our history has been interwoven with that of Europe for a thousand years and more. It was no mere coincidence that the European names of

---

9   An extract from 'Epitaph on an Army of Mercenaries' by A E Houseman (1917). The poem was dedicated to the 'Old Comptemptibles', the professional British Army of 1914 before the advent of Kitchener's 'New Army' of volunteers.

10   The first major action of the British forces in WW1 which inspired a popular legend – the *Angels of Mons* – about a group of angels who protected the British Army during their retreat.

Eisenhower and Montgomery led the invading forces to the liberation of France in June 1944.

Despite the distractions of the outbreak of war, I had completed my examination ordeals by the end of August and was ready and eager to dodge the distributors of white feathers in London's West End and to succumb to the ubiquitous image of Kitchener urging that King and Country needed us.[11]

A second regiment of Sharpshooters under a brother of Sir Douglas Haig was forming at St John's Wood and this I joined within hours of completing my last *viva voce* exam. It was a marked contrast. Not only had the Royal Horse gunners disappeared to France and Bolster, Bronco and Boudicea been replaced by very different kind of horse-flesh from the shafts of the London buses; but the careful regimental authorities of the Regular Army had handed in all the normal equipment of the barracks and we were left without pail, broom or shovel with which to cleanse the now highly smelling stables.

'Come on, lads!' said one hard-bitten ex-Queens Bay NCO 'What is the matter with your 'ands? It's good clean 'orse-shit'. Clean, it may have been, in his way of looking at it, but still it reeked very strongly. As water was being husbanded for the horses and a wash was hard to get, one's meals were very different from those in the Lyons Popular[12] which I had been snatching between the rapid fire of the Examiners.

The First Battle of Ypres was developing critically and reinforcements were called for urgently in France. Since the Second Sharpshooters regiment was being trained as a reserve unit, I was eager to join the First Regiment now stationed near Wallingford in Berkshire and currently training in mass tactics on the Berkshire Downs with the remainder of the London Mounted Division.

A scheme had been introduced earlier by which Territorials were able to opt for overseas service in lieu of purely home

11 White feathers were distributed by women in the streets to shame men who were not in uniform.
12 J Lyons & Co, a popular London restaurant chain, founded in 1884. The last of the famous Lyons Corner House teashops closed in 1977.

defence duties. This option, which I had accepted, now stood me in good stead and enabled me to transfer to my old comrades in Berkshire; but the obstacles to reaching France still persisted.

About that moment the Germans created a diversion by moving a lot of empty transport shipping in the Elbe, and the War Office responded by strengthening the coastal defence forces in Norfolk, where Sandringham and a 'steep-to' shore formation were supposed to offer attractions for a landing to the Enemy. So the London Mounted troops which had been destined for the northerly sector of the line in Flanders found themselves, instead, sleeping on the hard hard pavements of Reading and Cromer at either end of a long hungry cross-country trek to East Anglia. There was a complete breakdown in the commissariat so that for twenty-four hours our only sustenance consisted of raw mangolds raided from the fields along the railway line when the train loitered or halted.

In the coastwise villages, however, things were orderly and realistic and all arms were held on instant alert, day and night. Every now and then some alarm was given, usually it seemed to us on the coldest and stormiest nights and we found ourselves in rapidly donned uniform patrolling the cliffs at a sharp trot and breathing curses on the imaginative staff who had called us out in such conditions.

Grindstones were requisitioned from the farmers and a ferocious edge given to our cavalry sabres; these were put to test in practice squadron charges across the level sandy beaches, resulting in a steadily growing number of earless horses.

But the novelty of it all soon wore off and once again the gnawing fear of missing the war began to develop. It was in these circumstances that, shortly after Christmas 1914, I received a letter posting me to a temporary commission in one of the Kitchener battalions of the Essex Regiment and directing me to report to them at Colchester by a certain date. Here then was the opportunity to get cracking and, it must be admitted, the prospect of becoming an officer held definite attractions compared with the scope of a Number 3, horse-holder, the very lowest form of cavalry life.

Armed with the letter, I presented myself at CO's Orders; but my appreciation of the situation was not very good. The fiery old Colonel was nothing if not a cavalryman and as such, fretting to be up and at 'em. He read me a pithy lecture on the mistakes being made in denuding the French front of mounted troops, the uselessness of infantry generally and of Kitchener's brand of upstart infantry in particular. I retired defeated but persisted in presenting myself with my letter again for the next few days until I was positively forbidden to appear any more.

In the course of these histrionics the colonel had declared that I should blankety-blank-well have to walk to Colchester if I really wanted to become a footslogger. After brooding over all that I personally, and the army and the country were missing, that is exactly what I decided to do. It was not difficult in uniform to thumb a lift on the considerable amount of military transport that filled the eastern roads and I had much satisfaction in trundling past the colonel's forbidden headquarters building under a tarpaulin in a limbered waggon[13], appropriately enough, belonging to an infantry unit.

By many expedients I arrived eventually at Hyderabad Barracks, Colchester, to receive a daunting reception from the Adjutant: 'Oh! You're Banks, are you? Well we've just had word that you are posted as a deserter, so you'd better see the Old Man.' Colonels everywhere: but this was a very different character from the cavalry martinet. After examining my letter and listening to my story, he told me that he sympathised with the Yeomanry Colonel's feelings:

> It seems a pity to set up an entirely fresh organisation and not use the Territorial Army. But Lord Kitchener thinks it is going to be a long war; and he may well turn out to be right. In any case we shall need all arms and no one of them is going to win alone. Come along and have some tea with me and the missus.

---

13 The detachable front of a gun carriage.

Thus I found myself rapidly translated from a semi-hunted fugitive into the amiable atmosphere of a homely tea-party. And at the end the Colonel said: 'Only the War Office can decide whether you are to be shot at dawn for desertion or made a Field Marshal. So you must go and see them, and you can take a letter from me that I shall be very happy to have you in the 44th if they decide that way.'

So I made my way to Whitehall and for weeks reported daily in the interminable corridors of the War Office.

While I was back in London I learnt that I had scored highly enough in the Civil Service examination in August to be offered a place in the Indian Civil Service or a Colonial Cadetship; but neither of these seemed then to hold much for the future and only comparatively unattractive posts were available at home. So, while the authorities debated my immediate fate, I weighed one future against another and decided finally to wait and see how the war worked it out for me.

The first intervention of Fate favoured the Infantry: an announcement in the *London Gazette* made an honest soldier of me again and sent me travelling back to Colchester in the uniform of a Second Lieutenant and wearing with pride the badges of the Essex Regiment.[14]

In the Orderly Room at Hyderabad Barracks I might have risen from the dead. But I found a hearty reception awaiting me when I reported to D Company and discovered that it was skippered by Captain Wyeth[15], a well-beloved schoolmaster who had commanded the OTC at Elizabeth College, Guernsey and

14 The *London Gazette* shows that DB was appointed temporary 2nd Lieutenant on 5 Dec, cancelled on 18 Dec and reinstated on 29 Dec 1914.
15 Reverend Captain Frank John Sadler Wyeth (1878-1953) was a schoolmaster at Elizabeth College 1904-1911. In addition to teaching chemistry, he commanded the Officer Training Corps, and employed his scientific skills as States Analyst for the States of Guernsey. In 1911, he was appointed headmaster of Newport Grammar School in Essex. He joined the 10th Essex Regiment in 1914, was awarded the Military Cross in 1916, and was twice mentioned in dispatches. After demobilisation he returned to his job as headmaster in Newport, a position which he held until his retirement in 1938.

was pulling some powerful strings to officer his new unit. Thus, all unwitting, I had been summoned from the dreary chores of horse-holding to the greater potentialities of the New Army. This, indeed, was part of the selective process which was going on all over the country – a vast exercise in nepotism, one might say. But at least it was one that attenuated the concentrated holocausts of leadership like the Public Schools' Battalion: 'the Spring of the year that lay buried in France'.

Already installed in the happy Company were Willie Hunt, a junior master from the Newport Grammar School, Tommy Thompson, a short and lovable budding London lawyer, Hawkins, frail, dogged and scholarly and John Howitt, a poetic person who might well have graced the ranks of the pop-singers of a later era.

Alongside the neighbouring companies, one of which was imbued with the worship of efficiency to the point of emulating the habit of the Prussian military (or maybe the other New Army of Cromwell's time) of cropping their heads, we seemed almost painfully unwarlike. But there are different ways of achieving the objectives of corporate action – one by the automatic response of close discipline, the other by the winning of the heart and the corresponding response of the head to what is required. I am not persuaded, after long and varied observation, which is the better. No doubt every leader uses a certain degree of each. But there is equally no doubt that with D Company the formula of winning the heart paid off handsomely in the testing fires of active service still to come.

Ian Hay's play *The First Hundred Thousand,* which was appearing at this time in *Blackwood's Magazine,* paints a picture which sufficiently resembled our experiences for us to subscribe to the monthly issues and, as an alternative to other military lectures, we would read and discuss these with the men in the barrack rooms.[16] The results were invariably revealing, not

16 Ian Hay was the pen name of Major General John Hay Beith, best-known as a prolific novelist and playwright. *The First Hundred Thousand* (published in 1915) – a lighthearted fictional account of Lord Kitchener's volunteer army during the first year of WW1 – was an instant best seller.

merely because this early form of 'teach-in' was obviously more entertaining than 'At-the-halt-on-the-left-form-platoon' but because, for almost the first time, the barriers of rank and class and the many stratifications of social life and civil organisation were traversed and mutual understanding established. One found the men always eager to talk about their own experiences and circumstances. Perhaps they were not so greatly interested in happenings outside their own sphere, which is only natural. So one would draw them on to talk about their families and their occupations. The latter called for some care, for I was warned by the company sergeant-major that there were one or two cases which required delicate probing. When I asked the sergeant-major confidentially about one fellow, who appeared to be principally employed on evening work and to have had frequent periods of holiday, he turned out to have been a professional burglar, and well-known to the police!

Gradually one built up the backcloth of humble homes against which this phenomenal flowering of patriotism comes spontaneously to our nation at times such as these:

> Immortal in each little street,
> The soul in its integrity.[17]

The greatest handicap was the loss of dignity and pride involved in the wretched convict-like blue uniforms which at first were all that were available to issue to the flood of volunteers who poured into the New Army. To help to overcome this the platoons clubbed together to buy a khaki set for communal wear when the turn came to go home on weekend leave. It didn't always fit well but it was a popular performance kitting out Shorty or Lofty to dazzle the ladies of Wapping. And no regimental sergeant-major of the Guards ever inspected a uniform more closely than his comrades when the returning wearer delivered it back on Sunday night.

---

17 An extract from the poem 'London 1940' by AA Milne. He wrote this poem sitting on the steps to his house, the rest of which had been destroyed during an air raid.

It was a busy, absorbing, life – teaching and learning – the rudiments of soldiering. Someone had warned that no military unit of any size could be readied for battle in less than a year; but Kitchener and the authorities were determined to have us in the field in 1915, and that in divisional formations or larger. A very remarkable achievement, as it turned out.

In the repeat performance in 1939 reliance was placed on the expansion of the Territorial Army and, as a result, some divisions were made serviceable within months. Now, in 1963, with the crass mutilation of the Territorials something has been thrown away which we shall not easily replace.[18] May one hope and pray that there will be no third performance.

By May 1915 we had completed the main elements of our drill and musketry, had marched over a hundred miles in full marching order, bivouacking or billeting nightly on the way through Suffolk and subsequently moved by road and train to newly erected encampments in the Wylye Valley on the borders of Salisbury Plain.

Eleven weeks was the allotted time for the final intensive training in Wiltshire. In July King George V reviewed the Division on the rolling sward near Stonehenge.

The King sent us a message:-

> You are about to join your comrades at the Front in bringing to a successful end this relentless war of nearly twelve months' duration.
>
> Your prompt patriotic answer to the Nation's Call to Arms will never be forgotten. The keen exertions of all ranks have brought you to a state of efficiency not unworthy of my Regular Army.
>
> I am confident that in the field you will nobly uphold the traditions of the fine regiments whose name you bear.
>
> In bidding you farewell, I pray that God may bless you in all your undertakings.

18 Compulsory National Service was gradually phased out between 1957 and 1963. As a result, the Territorial Army was reorganised, reducing the number of fighting units from 266 to 195.

To which General Maxse[19] replied:-

> I beg you will convey to His Majesty our unalterable devotion to his Person and to his Throne and our determination to uphold the best traditions of the British Army in war.

Remembering a duplicated experience, with somewhat varied words, in 1940 with the 50th Division departing for France after review by George VI in the Cotswolds, it all seems to have a familiar sequence: the *ave Caesar, morituri te salutant*[20], the drawbridge goes down and you are across the moat with the portcullis banged behind and out on your own.

As you step ashore on the other side, you imagine a campaign medal and perhaps one or two more blossoming on your breast. But more prosaically, you realise your pay has taken a beneficent bound under that paradoxical dispensation of the British Army called Field Allowance, by which one is paid a good deal more in circumstances in which expenses are considerably less.

On July 25th 1915 the last parade in England took place and the battalion marched forth along the road to Wylye station, where it entrained for Folkestone. We descended the cutting to the harbour – where so many trod on the way to the battlefields that Folkestone later planted it with rosemary – and sailed over the Channel to Boulogne.

We disembarked at Boulogne just after midnight with the rain pouring down in torrents and the first acquaintance with the wet *pavé* was none too pleasant. Everyone had had his heavy boots nailed in readiness for campaigning and more than one man went down full-length on the cobbles. A long pull up the steep hill to the rest camp at the top left the unit exhausted, but a bright sun in the morning and the novelty of the surroundings

---

19 General Sir Frederick Ivor Maxse (1862-1958) – a WW1 general best known for his innovative training methods. In 1915, he was the commanding officer of the 18th Division, to which the 10th Essex Regiment belonged.
20 Hail Caesar, those who are about to die salute you.

Family diary entry for Sunday, July 11, 1915:
"Don home from Cotswolds. Tea in the field. Photos by
Bramley in the evening. The motor a great success".
Above (L to R): Blanche, Margaret, Thomas senior,
Frank Brownsey, Donald & Maurice.
Below (L to R): Donald in 2nd Lt uniform, Margaret,
Thomas senior. Standing (L to R): Maurice, Blanche.

soon had the men chirping about like sparrows among the local children who thronged around the camp.

''Ark, Bill' said one, 'Even the little buggers speak French!'

After an early breakfast we marched down to the town to entrain, swinging along well to the strains of our village band from Wivenhoe, and the inhabitants lined the streets full of enthusiasm, much as I remember they did when the Guards marched in from Dover along the same streets in 1939.

A fat lady was heard to remark: 'Good marchaires, bad fightaires.' 'Arf a mo', missis' replied one cockney. 'Give us a chawnce. We ain't started yet.'

As the long military train meandered into the French countryside there was considerable speculation about our destination. Ypres was the favourite bet, but the German attacks there had died down and from the comparatively peaceful rural scenes through which we went, it was apparent that it was to be a different fate and a new area.

With the frustration of the enemy outflanking attempt at Ypres there were fears of pressure developing at the eastern end of the long trench line. The French had requested the British to take over more frontage to release concentrations for the future struggle at Verdun. The tranche agreed upon was the area around Amiens, later to be famous under the battle-name of the Somme; and thither were we bound.

*2nd Lieutenant T M Banks
in the trenches near La Boisselle, 1915.*

3
THE SOMME

The area of the battlefields of the Somme is roughly equal to the county of Wiltshire, which it also resembles in topography and extent. Within this area, on a frontage of some 15 miles protruding westward like an elbow in the north-south front, from where the trench line crossed the River Somme and its marshes above Amiens to the higher ground near Arras, took place the great assault of 1st July 1916: an encounter which claimed 60,000 British lives on that one day. From then on during a period of nine months of continuous struggle, about 500,000 British troops were killed or wounded (compared with some 15,000 at Waterloo, 14,000 at Alamein and 80,000 Japanese killed by the atom bomb at Hiroshima). This holocaust involving half-a-million souls, together with a similar total of losses by the enemy, took place in that ravaged land of Picardy – not much larger than an English county.

At the time we first knew it, however, it was a comparatively peaceful landscape of rolling chalk downs, punctuated by woods, which yielded reasonably good trenches in mixed chalk and mud according to the vagaries of the weather. Behind the line small picturesque villages were scattered, providing friendly billets when we were not in action. Amiens, Arras and Albert were the main centres of population; they were never wholly deserted by their gallant and tenacious inhabitants throughout all the trials and tribulations which befell them through the four years of war, and afforded grateful diversions for the troops from the asperities of active service.

The earlier operations of 1914-15 had left this part of Northern France relatively unscathed as the German Army swept past in the Schlieffen Plan and rashly ignored the opportunities of reaching the coast. Here and there, mainly athwart the main roads leading westward, there were evidences of desperate fights and heavy losses by the gallant French rearguards. In one such place at the village of La Boisselle across the Bapaume Road to Albert we found many buried bodies of French soldiers in the old and famous long blue coats and *pantalons rouges* of the historic past.[1]

At one point at the entrance to a long communication trench leading to the front line time and the weather had combined to preserve in a semi-fossilised state the arm and hand of one brave *piou-piou*,[2] projecting from the parapet. It was an article of faith that we should all shake hands with him for luck before passing by; and in this macabre way we saluted the warriors of those earlier fights in their Valhalla – *morts pour la Patrie*.

The fighting here had been so fiercely contested that the respective lines still remained only a few yards apart. The low murmurs of the German sentries and the rattle of their kit could be heard as with bated breath we occupied the outposts of our own trenches. Fortunately, an unwritten convention mutually prohibited the throwing of hand-grenades and woe betide the breach of this unofficial truce; then hell was let loose and vengeance exacted by the artillery of both sides upon the areas behind.

Except when the Germans sent over some heavy and very frightening mortar fire or were unusually active in the insidious mining warfare that went on underground, there was quite a matey spirit between the front areas and climatic troubles were shared fraternally. Some of the Germans spoke English and used to shout questions about London, in particular about the Strand or the Savoy where they had been waiters in the pre-war days. In one raid on our lines some forerunner of Goebbels planted a banner bearing the words: 'Brave British Boys. Why will you fight for your bloated Capitalists who sit at home in armchairs and send you to death?'

---

1   In 1914, the French Army wore a traditional uniform of blue coats and red trousers, little changed since the Napoleonic era. It was blamed for the heavy losses at the start of the war, and by 1915 a less conspicuous dark blue uniform was introduced.
2   The French nickname for an infantry soldier, equivalent to the British term 'Tommy'.

On another occasion, when dugouts and trenches alike were crumbling in a sudden thaw, there was an unusual display of Teutonic humour in a notice on the enemy parapet:-

> Dear Sirs,
>   On and after the 15th inst. you can have these bloody trenches.
>
> Yours faithfully.

But all was not as suave and amiable as that for, deep down below in the bowels of the earth, both sides were busy in strange and esoteric subterranean struggles. The technique was to drive a main shaft, vertical or inclined, somewhere behind the front trench and preferably in dead ground where the extracted soil could be dumped unobserved. Horizontal saps were then driven out towards the enemy and, when the goal was reached, chambers at their extremities were hollowed out, filled with explosive and up they went.

I suspect that the British were the first to initiate this seemingly rather pointless form of warfare. Sapping and mining occupied a traditional place in the curriculum of the Royal Engineers, stretching back to the castles and linear fortifications of medieval times; but there had been little opportunity for their employment by the British Army for a hundred years or more. Now we had all gone back to a vast exercise of static warfare and anything which offered a solution to the deadlock of the trench lines seemed worth trying.

Whoever started it, the Germans were not slow to participate. So it had only to be discovered that one side had begun deep digging for a counter-effort to be set off by the other. Each of the mining works was then directed to forestall and blow up the other and groped in blindness for the unseen foe. It was a world of its own into which the denizens of the surface were only grudgingly admitted. On the occasions when I was allowed below, I was told that it was all right so long as you could hear tappings from the other side. So there was comfort in the sepulchral knocks which came mysteriously through the chalk.

If they stopped it meant that the German miners were piling in explosive. Then, either you had to race him with your own – a most hair-raising experience – or give up. Such was the talisman until someone introduced an automatic pick which knocked away unattended and enabled the explosive charge to be readied at the same time. The sappers condemned this emphatically as unsporting and their nice cosy troglodyte life was never the same again.

We used to meet these rugged little Welsh miners hurrying through our trenches bearing their canaries, but gave little thought to them until the ground quivered like a minor earthquake and erupted like a volcano in unexpected places. On one occasion the enemy's countermeasures had caused a shortfall and I emerged from my company headquarters to find a vast mountain crater, like some weird moonscape where our old front trench had run. There, on the forward lip where his command post formerly stood, was little Tommy Thompson and the unburied portion of his platoon, gallantly poised on the new earthworks unexpectedly provided, and ready to defend our new possessions to the last if the enemy recovered his equanimity sooner than we did. Little, indeed, seemed to have been gained and the tacit *entente* suffered a shattering set-back. But the sappers were pleased as they said it enabled them to check their positions, or whatever they termed their subterranean navigation, and they continued steadfastly to push their saps under the most dangerous German machine-gun sites in preparation for the great assault.

It is not known definitely why the Somme Sector was selected by Haig for this vast enterprise. Strategically, there were no particularly desirable features to be taken and though, as a cavalryman, the nature of the country might have attracted him in the hope of a breakthrough, we saw little in the way of such preparations. Instead, we were bitterly disappointed when, having pierced the German Line at Montauban there were no reserves available to exploit success. Most probably, the decision hinged on the fact that the River Somme formed the boundary between the French and British Armies who were to attack jointly in the Western sector in order to relieve the mounting pressure on the French reserves at Verdun where the bitter struggle had raged since February 1916.

We were vaguely conscious of the mutual effort. After the French battalions in their new horizon-blue uniforms departed for eastern France, their gunners arrived with their antediluvian howitzers from the 1870 War and, strangely enough, other heavy pieces dismounted from the fortresses of Verdun: all with the intention of supplementing the cascade of explosives raining down on the enemy lines. We felt drawn closer together and embraced in the spirit of *On les aura*.[3]

However, there was however scant time for such thoughts as the tempo of the preparations heightened and the crescendo of the guns deafened us in the woods where we bivouacked before the march up the communication trenches into the front line at Carnoy (I have never heard properly since that time). Then came that first experience of the 'dreary, doubtful waiting hours Before the brazen battle fury starts.'[4] Afterwards, with repeated experience, this became almost a routine.

In our little company headquarters, hollowed out of the parapet we had shortly to climb, we were perhaps a little more conscious of tension than later, after we had experienced many other Zero Hours as old campaigners. Yet, except for the incessant rumble of our own guns there was surprisingly little drama about this all-consuming moment. Thompson was studying his Palgrave's *Golden Treasury* which he had brought up in his haversack and Howitt was writing on a field pad the poem which follows at the end of this chapter.

The men crouched in the trenches on either side of us were quiet and thoughtful, but cheered up when we went to them

---

3   Refers to a famous French propaganda poster, designed by Abel Faivre and issued in 1915 by the French government, asking people to subscribe to a loan in support of the war. It shows a young soldier with arm raised and gun in hand, urging his companions forward into battle with the words 'On les aura' [We will have them].

4   Excerpt from 'Into Battle' by Julian Grenfell (1915).

and the beneficent rum ration was distributed. Then the great moment: 'Fix Bayonets! Over the Top! Good Old Essex and the best of Luck!' And over we went.

Out in the distance on the right the scattered line of the East Surreys were dribbling forward a football. I thought of that when England were declared winners at Wembley in the World Cup many years later.

On the left the Royal Berkshires were plodding through some telling machine-gun fire from an emplacement which our Company was subsequently ordered to subdue with grenades.

For the rest it was very much like one of our many practices, except for the din and the dust of the barrage ahead, the explosion of the long-prepared mine saps and a strange way in which a man here and there would suddenly trip and fall, as if he had caught his foot in an obstacle. I was almost oblivious to being a target and to the fact that the air was full of bullets until a little mongrel dog ran across to me out of the enemy lines; as I bent down to pat its head, it wagged its tail and fell dead with a bullet through it. Like the permutations of a football pool, the bullet that has your number on it is at long, long odds.

Despite that bit of *ex post facto* philosophy, however, one reached the shelter of the German front line trenches and their surrendering occupants with some relief. There was much still to do as our objectives lay deep in their reserve system and all the difficult ritual of leap-frogging 'mopping-up' remained to be carried out. Although pulverised by our seven-day bombardment, the Germans still fought hard; it was a long slogging day, hand in hand with the Royal Berkshires, before we penetrated the successive systems and many of the gun positions and finally were through.

Alas! The necessary reserves to exploit the unexpected break-through by the 18th Division were not available and a great opportunity was lost. And alas! the end of the second day found me on a stretcher with a badly-injured ankle on the way to the Base Hospital at Wimereux and thence by crowded hospital ship across the Channel again to Southampton.

Before The Attack

I've a feeling in my stomach, just as though I hadn't eaten,
Though I've scoffed my bully less than two hours back.
I've a chill in all my bones which no
    blooming sun could heaten,
For I've got to go across and do my whack.

Yus! It may be fine attacking , but it isn't fun just sitting,
Just sitting still and waiting, in a bluddy, muddy 'ole,
Till the gunners lift their barrage. Gawd!
    ain't the Sergeant spitting,
Fit to sicken anybody with a bit or two of soul.

Struth! he ain't so mighty lively, tho' he's
    standing there and laffing
With our gaudy little orficer, wot's a proper kinder sport
But even he, I'm betting, would give
    something to be chaffing
A bit of Piccadilly wot's no better than she ought.

The guns are still agoin' like a rolling burst of thunder,
Same as if the clouds were fighting in their anger overhead;
And I do not want to do it, but cannot 'elp but wonder
Wo 'appens, really 'appens, to those
    'eaps of bones – the dead.

Oh! I know the parson's preaching when
    we're resting back in billets
And 'e talks to us of 'Eaven, as 'e must to draw 'is pay.
But it don't seem somehow natural that
    we'll turn to angels sudden
In some draughty marble palace. Still
    it may work out that way.
Lawdy! Just to think of Bill there, or old Nobby gaily
    winging

Through the golden 'alls of 'Eaven.
    Why! I'd go there just to see.
And the joke is that I may do when the
    'eavies stop their singing
And I've got to give old Fritz 'is chance
    of plugging dear old me.

John L D Howitt

'Mud impeded the assembly, soaked and chilled the men
during their long wait, trapped every step in the assault,
clogged rifles and cut off rations and communications.'

Passchendaele (Imperial War Museum)

4

PASSCHENDAELE &
BACKS TO THE WALL

M y ankle injury, though it was painful and disabling, was what was currently termed a 'Blighty'. In other words, it took you back out of the hurly-burly to the pleasant fleshpots of home and removed you providentially from the roulette wheels of the casualty lists which were spinning distinctly unfavourably in our unit at this period. One felt all the time a bit of a truant and missed the comradeship of high endeavour. But there were weighty compensations in the green, green countryside and the immense peacefulness of the hospital at Osborne House, in the Isle of Wight.[1] The house, with its sorrowful relics of the Prince Consort, remained untouched since he died and still sacrosanct by Victoria's command. Years later, I was privileged to visit another royal residence across the Channel, Le Hardelot, where Princess Louise[2] had similarly imposed a freeze upon the relics of her husband, the Duke of Argyll, down to the very ink imprints in the blotter on the desk where he was last writing.

> Death lays its icy hand on Kings.[3]

It was not long before I was able to hobble about and report in due course to the Essex Reserve Battalion at Felixstowe. My recollections of England during this time are not very distinct. The country appeared to have accepted the prospect of a long war and was facing up to it with practical equanimity. Rationing was a novelty; but to be attacked itself by the Zeppelins, arriving over the east coast, and by daylight in the City, when Fokkers[4]

---

1   Queen Victoria's favourite residence.
2   See Chapter 9
3   From the poem 'Death the Leveller' by James Shirley (1596-1666).
4   In 1915 the first fighter plane armed with a synchronised machine gun.

damaged the Central Telegraph Office: that was outrageous. I was in the Savoy Restaurant when some small bombs were dropped on the Embankment near Cleopatra's Needle. Although dinner went on uninterrupted, the atmosphere was one of intense indignation. These were indeed some of the first manifestations of the belief that Britain rightfully owned her airspace and was determined to be Master of the Air as well as Ruler of the Waves.

On the way through London I called in at the General Post Office to see how matters stood for my future Civil Service career. I was kindly received by the Second Secretary who was no little surprised to see what was just a name on an examination list limping into his room in uniform. He told me that there were some vacancies as assistant surveyors in the provinces but he would advise me to wait for a headquarters job if I was prepared to do so. As the latter meant £50 a year more, I elected that choice, remembering acutely the austerity of former years. So it was that fate steered my halting footsteps eventually to St Martin's le Grand.

At Felixstowe we seemed to alternate between dispersing on the golf course to dodge the Zeppelin bombs and the distasteful duties of handling conscientious objectors. One particular tough case refused even to stand up, so he had to be strapped to a stretcher and up-ended in the presence of the commanding officer. The technique of non-violence and sit-ins has been much developed since then, but it made one think!

By February 1917 I had rejoined the 10th Essex on the Somme – by then a vast morass of chalky mud. They had added the notable actions of Delville Wood and Thiepval to their credit since I had left and were very hardened warriors, with many familiar faces missing. It was not long before I was over the top again, this time in a snow-storm and clothed in white nightgowns as an element of concealment. A minor wound in the thigh from a rifle-grenade and a Military Cross were the fruits of this fight and I began to feel that I had regained respectability.[5]

---

5   The citation reads: 'For conspicuous gallantry and devotion to duty. He led the left assaulting company in a most gallant manner, and succeeded in

By this time the enemy had had enough of the loss of men, ground and morale and withdrew by stages to a segment of the vast trench-works, known as the Hindenburg Line[6] which they had constructed across the base of their remaining segment of the Somme. As they withdrew, the Germans booby-trapped liberally: a new phenomenon which did them little credit. To put explosive under an inviting bottle of wine or in an armchair in a vacated headquarters, a trip-wire to a bomb in a dark dugout or to wire up a latrine with detonators seemed unworthy of good soldiers.

Our days on the Somme were now at an end, at least for the time being. New dawns awaited us, first at Arras, where we were among the first to break into the Hindenburg Line. In the best German tradition this was truly *Wunderbar*. The trenches were so wide that they in themselves constituted tank traps and were duplicated throughout by a vast timber-lined underground system, lit by electricity, and proofed against gas: a prototype of the sort of troglodyte existence which perhaps is in store for mankind in the days of nuclear warfare. There were even miniature underground railways running within and along the many miles of this prodigious rabbit warren.

But we were not destined to remain long in this enervating atmosphere of luxurious pseudo-safety. By the middle of 1917 we were bound north for the scene of so much earlier trouble around Ypres.

Much has been written by later military historians and critics on the errors of Haig in launching and, particularly, in continuing the muddy massacre of the Third Battle of Ypres, commonly known now as the Battle of Passchendaele. With the benefit of hindsight a considerable case against it can be made. But those who were there and who were exposed to all the rigours and ordeals from July 1917 until the end of the year are disinclined to criticise the concept or to condemn the leadership. Nor in all

capturing his objective in spite of strong hostile opposition.' (*Supplement to the London Gazette*, 26 April, 1917, p.3934).

6   The Hindenburg Line (*Siegfriedstellung*) was a German defensive position built during the winter of 1916-17 from Arras to Lafftaux in Eastern France.

that time have I any record or recollection of complaint from the troops. I did once overhear a conversation in a watery shell-hole: 'What was you before the war, Bert?' and the answer: ''Appy!'

In addition, as Christmas 1917 approached, too, some rather badly managed leave arrangements caused an element of unwonted sourness in the ranks. And when a German sergeant-major stumbled by mistake into a concrete pill-box that we had just captured near Houlthust Forest and produced some leave vouchers for himself to Germany, there were some exceptionally caustic remarks.

But, so far as my experience went, I do not think that morale suffered from the physical trials nor that Gough's retreat[7] of March 1918 in the south can properly be ascribed to that factor.

The broad idea of a sweep on to the higher ground above Ypres and along the Passchendaele Ridge towards the coast so as to threaten the German U-Boat bases on the Belgian Coast was attractive. There was also a general consciousness that the French Army, bleeding from its Verdun losses and suffering from the aftermath of the *Chemin des Dames*,[8] again needed support, whether or not (as has since been disputed) Foch requested it directly.[9]

The first great tragedy was the failure to make fast progress along the higher ground on the right flank. We attacked through the rain which set in on July 31 up the Ypres-Menin Road and without the benefit of the superb observation which the enemy had over the whole of our assembly area of Ypres. Although we threw him back from the lip of the hill, we found ourselves up against a very strong system of woods and pill-boxes developed in depth before we could approach the Passchendaele Ridge. Speed and ground were the two essentials of the problem: we

7 General Sir Hubert Gough (1870-1963), commander of the British Fifth Army 1916-18. The Fifth Army bore the brunt of the opening phase of the German Spring Offensive. Overwhelmingly outnumbered, the army suffered from a collapse of morale and retreated, resulting in Gough's dismissal.
8 The site of the Second Battle of the Aisne, a 12-day battle in April 1917 in which the French army suffered a major defeat with 271,000 casualties.
9 Marshal Ferdinand Foch, Commander-in-Chief of the Allied Armies, March 1918-January 1920.

were repeatedly defeated in our attempts to subdue the strong-points and suffered heavy losses among our officers. One in particular, a gallant fellow named Rex Compton, who had only heard a few days before of the death of his twin brother in a neighbouring Division, was mown down not far from me when he tried to rush a machine-gun at the corner of Inverness Copse across a hundred yards of open ground.[10]

The general effect was to divert the British efforts to the lower lying ground which lay like a saucer in the area below the features for which we were fighting; it was in this ghastly shell-churned expanse, with the streams and the land drainage shattered, that the worst of the subsequent muddy massacre took place.

Prodigies were performed by troops and staff alike in getting the guns forward, together with all the necessary munitions. For the most part, they had to be man-handled along miles of duck boards, none too securely laid, across the waterlogged morasses.

The outstanding achievement of our battalion in these conditions was an attack on a stubbornly held square mile or so of broken trees and bricks on a slight eminence, which had once been the unassuming Flemish village of Poelcapelle. There had already been a number of thwarted British attempts to wrest this position from the enemy. But, in consonance with the general trend of all the operations at that moment, the more the place defied us, the more determined both sides became. I suppose there was some of the spirit of Waterloo about Wellington's 'Hard pounding, Gentlemen!' and success to him who could stand the most of it.

The assembly involved a long plod of about four miles up the duck-board tracks which spanned the featureless wilderness of mud, with our batteries belching out at sudden intervals and shelled in turn by the German guns. Gas shells alternated with the heavy crumps and with gas: a man wearing a helmet would slip off the duck-boards and the line would have to halt while he

---

10   2nd Lieut Rex Compton (1897-1917) was killed in action on 12 August 1917. His brother, 2nd Lieut Guy Compton, 9th Royal Sussex Regiment, was killed on 27 July 1917. However, they were not twins – Guy was three years older than Rex.

was rescued from drowning in the mud. The battalion, carrying its own weapons and ammunition on its back, was strung out in single file over nearly a mile; and the trudge was a truly agonising experience, not alleviated by the realisation that if you were wounded the only prospect of haven was to find the way back over the same penitential route. At the culmination of the approach march were the isolated concrete pill-boxes captured earlier from the enemy, the only features of an otherwise complete abomination of desolation and under steady fire from well-registered German guns. Here we set up our battle headquarters, shared in this instance with the Norfolks who attacked with us. The scene within made an arresting picture.

Imagine a place about ten feet by twelve, not much larger than the average sitting room, but low-roofed and windowless. Into this crowded some 60 human beings: colonels, adjutants, liaison officers, signallers, runners, stretcher-bearers and doctors, with all their paraphernalia – pigeons, buzzers, medical stores, a wireless transmitter in one corner, a primus stove going in another – all lit by two or three spluttering candles. Round about, and on the top, shells were bursting intermittently. A sentry was killed by one before our eyes as he stood sheltering in the doorway at my elbow, and the force of the shells exploding would blow the candles out repeatedly.

This was the nerve-centre of the battle on our front: round it all day pulsated the news of how things were going. Runners brought in word of the capture of the main objectives, running the gauntlet of the shells and arriving breathless and exhausted. The exceptional conditions led to the use of pigeons for communication; they at least could surmount the mudfields and, flying back from advanced positions to their divisional dovecotes, would often bring immediate news to Higher Command who buzzed it forward to the battalion – an unusual inversion of affairs.

The night of waiting was the worst I can remember. Inside the pill-box there was comparative warmth and safety. But the men had neither: they waited, soaked to the skin and cowering in shallow, watery shell-slits until the early light when, labouring and struggling through the awful mud, they followed through

42

where the Norfolks had started the attack and triumphantly reached the higher ground by the village.

One noteworthy feature, which showed that the Higher Command was not entirely deficient in imagination, was the deployment of General Maxse's 'Chinese Army': a lot of dummy figures on poles used to divert the enemy fire and distract attention from a flanking movement.

Apart from the rigours of the approach and of our bombarded headquarters, my main recollection of those memorable twenty-four hours was the sheer physical exhaustion of getting across the uncharted mud to the points we had won, or which were threatened by counterattack. In the evening one such enemy attack was made in strength up the Westroosebeke Road. Happily, this could be seen in preparation for some time. Happily for us, too, the enemy seemed unable to face advancing across the naked mudfields as we had done and confined itself to the narrow frontage of the road where it was easier for us to concentrate our fire and repulse the attack.

Poelcapelle had cost the Essex two hundred and fifty casualties – a quarter of its strength. But it was an outstanding victory, wrested from that inexorable opponent, General Mud, ensconced in his home country, Flanders. Mud impeded the assembly, soaked and chilled the men during their long wait, trapped every step in the assault, clogged rifles and cut off rations and communications. But, do its worst, it failed to quench the indomitable spirit of British soldiery.

Those trying days were followed by the blissful relief of another trip back across the Channel when I found myself detached from dangerous duties and posted to Aldershot for a course of training at the Senior Officers' School.

It was now commonly accepted that there was little hope of an early finish to the war and vast preparations of every kind were afoot to prepare for the Great Offensive of 1919. A very acceptable one, so far as we surviving veterans were concerned, was the preservation and cultivation of future leaders in the light of the heavy ravages in the earlier stages of the war.

General Kentish was one of the great exponents of this build-up and in his methods might be said to have foreshadowed the famous 'Binge' of Field Marshal Montgomery in the Second World War.[11] A particular stunt of his (that we considered particularly underhand) was to order an especially early morning parade of officers and then surreptitiously arrange for batmen and mess staff to be unavailable. The parade was then narrowly inspected by the general for cleaned buttons and Sam Brownes,[12] on the do-it-yourself principle; a watchful eye was also kept on the mess to determine the relative resourcefulness of future commanding officers in providing for their own breakfasts. The stunt led to remarkable results when it was launched on the first course; but its very success caused such consternation throughout the Army that, when posted to Aldershot, we became more concerned with the strategems of Kentish than the machinations of the Kaiser. I remember my room-mate Ian Bullough returning from weekend leave with complete breakfast rations for the coming week. They were packed by the fair hands of his lovely wife, Lily Elsie, who was then the popular theatre idol of London. Elaborate intelligence methods were set up to prepare against potential sudden shortages in batmen, boot polish, Brasso and Bronco;[13] but it was all a good enough exchange for the beastliness of Flanders. The massing of the German hordes on the St Quentin front, released by the Russian collapse, was regarded as not much more than a newspaper story.

However, on March 21, 1918, the reality of this became apparent. The breakthrough to Amiens on the Fifth Army front, known as the March 1918 Retreat, with its threat of dividing the Allied armies on the line of the Somme, sent us scuttling back to our units without further worries about batmen-less parades.

11 Brigadier-General Reginald Kentish (1876-1956) was the founder of the Senior Officers' School in 1916 to create a coherent training plan for army officers.

12 The 'Sam Browne' was a wide leather belt, supported by a narrower strap passing diagonally over the right shoulder, which had been a key feature of British Army officers' uniform since the Boer War.

13 *Brasso* was a liquid cleaner used to polish brass – especially uniform buttons. *Bronco* refers to a brand of toilet paper similar to tracing paper!

I managed to locate the 10th Essex as they withdrew from a spirited rear guard action east of Amiens. They had been reduced to the size of a company, with only four officers left; as they trudged along with a small herd of cows, led by the rear files, which had been recruited amid the chaos to provide milk and meat when rations and all else failed: an even better lesson in resourcefulness than the Senior Officers' School had afforded.

Lloyd George[14] by now had got a grasp on the situation. He appointed Foch as Generalissimo to the Allied armies and was pouring out reinforcements from home. A few hectic days in quiet billets near Amiens ensued while we hurriedly absorbed these new units. To my special interest, I found that some of them had been cycling up and down in defence of the East Anglian coast ever since I had taken the bit in my teeth in 1914 and opted for something more strenuous. I was told that I was a bit caustic in my welcome to them.

The Australians at Villers-Bretonneux were holding the eastern high ground covering Amiens under severe pressure. This was the moment, as I was able to describe at the ANZAC Day parade in Melbourne years later, of their superb night bayonet charge – a spectacular sight with the naked steel glittering in the moonlight and the phosphorous smoke and bursting shells. But the enemy were outflanking them at Hangard Wood and, together with the famous French Foreign Legion Division, we were ordered to their support. This was the only occasion on which I actually fought shoulder to shoulder with the French: it was a rich experience of contrasting tactics and temperament.[15]

---

14   David Lloyd George (1863-1945), Prime Minister of Britain 1916-22. At first, he was criticised for several military events. By spring, 1918, he showed a firmer hand.

15   DB was awarded the *Croix de Guerre* for this action. The citation reads: 'At Hangard Wood on the 25th and 26th April 1918, this officer showed the greatest gallantry and devotion to duty when in command of his Battalion, he personally patrolled in front of his Battalion in order to clear up an obscure situation and obtained valuable information, he rallied and led forward his men at a critical period, and by his personal courage, inspired all ranks. During this action he was twice slightly wounded (foot and arm), but remained at duty during the action, and his clothing was penetrated by a

At dawn a conventional set attack from tapes was launched across the wide shallow valley which separated us from the wood; when this came under heavy machine-gun fire the British slogged on, suffering and enduring their casualties. The French Spahis and Legionnaires,[16] on the other hand, would drop down to take cover and build up a new line from which they charged forward again with refreshed *élan*: '*L'Attaque, encore l'Attaque, toujours l'Attaque!*' It would be hard to say which were the more effective tactics, but each was in harmony with the national temperament and together they gained us the wood.

Inside, under the cover of the trees and undergrowth, the German techniques of cunning and concealment came into play; more than once I narrowly escaped being enticed into a well-contrived ambush. Miniature operations had to be extemporised to circumvent these tactics. During a conference with a French captain and one of my officers in the undergrowth, an enemy machine-gun caught the three of us together and in its traverse, killed the Frenchman with a bullet through the stomach and caught my lieutenant with a bad wound in the head. Between the two I was providentially odd man out. Binding up the head wound with a field dressing, I sent the British officer down to the rear with my runner and from that time onwards both disappeared.

After the war I was looking round a Business Efficiency Exhibition at Olympia[17] when a salesman from one of the stands came up to me and said he had a paper at home over my name to say that he was dead and, like Mark Twain, he thought it was grossly exaggerated.[18] What had happened was that, finding no trace of either man after the battle, we had assumed that they had been blown up on the way back and posted them as missing, believed killed. The runner had indeed been killed, but the officer

bullet on a third occasion.'

16 The Spahis were French cavalry regiments recruited from their colonies of Algeria, Tunisia and Morocco; Legionnaires were members of the French *Légion étrangère* (Foreign Legion) – a regiment of highly trained infantry soldiers open to any nationality.

17 The famous exhibition and conference centre in London's West Kensington was first opened in 1886.

18 Mark Twain famously said: 'The report of my death was an exaggeration.'

had struggled on until eventually he had been picked up by the French and evacuated by them down their medical network to a hospital on the Mediterranean. The head wound caused an amnesia which for many months left him incapable and it was not until that chance meeting at Olympia ten years later that the past could be fully reconstructed and the records adjusted.

Hangard, Villers-Bretonneux and, subsequently, a line of trenches extemporised across the main Albert–Amiens road overlooking our erstwhile billets in Albert (where the suspended Virgin and Child still leant precariously above the poor shattered town): these elements ultimately held back the advancing German armies from reaching Amiens. This was the time of Haig's stirring 'Backs to the Wall' Order of the Day (the counterpart to Petain's: '*Ils ne passeront pas*' at Verdun)[19]. As each dawn passed without new enemy efforts, we began to realise that British, French, Australians and the first American contingents who were now reaching us for battle-training had in truth established a durable barrier to the ambitious designs of Ludendorff.[20]

With the characteristic realism of Australians, when their gunners learnt of the legend of the war continuing so long as the leaning Virgin of Albert remained in place, they directed a few well-aimed shots around the Cathedral and removed that superstitious omen. And, true enough, from that time onwards our thoughts veered to the offensive. The tide had turned.

---

19 Issued from General Headquarters on 11 April 1918, Field Marshal Sir Douglas Haig's famous Special Order of the Day was the British Army's response to Germany's Spring Offensive – their last ditch attempt to push through to the Channel ports with the additional divisions released from the eastern front. It urges 'Victory will belong to the side which holds out the longest ... Every position must be held to the last man: there must be no retirement. With our backs to the wall and believing in the justice of our cause each one of us must fight on to the end.'

20 General Erich Ludendorff (1865-1937), Quartermaster-general of the German Army, and leader, along with Hindenburg, of the German WW1 campaign. He masterminded the Spring Offensive of 1918 (also known as the Ludendorff Offensive) which was seen as a strategic failure.

Major T M Banks MC, 10th Essex Regiment, c.1917

5

THE RETURN MATCH

In sporting parlance, the return match was to take place on the home ground – the Somme. The river, which runs from east to west, was to form the guide-line of the main spearhead into the positions of the enemy, which they had had scant time to consolidate. With the initiative in our hands, we attacked along the heights on either side – the British and some new Americans on the north bank with the Australians and Canadians on the south. The broad obstacle of the Somme marshes restricted the Germans' freedom to reinforce and added value to our growing superiority in morale.

During the next weeks we, as well as the enemy, were being misled by skilfully spread rumours which formed part of a giant deception plan. (This was the first instance of the ruses employed so successfully in the Second World War before launching the D-Day operations on the Normandy Coast.) Hitherto the attitude of Higher Command (mirrored all the way down through the ranks) tended to find something slightly degrading in concealment, camouflage and subterfuge. Now whispers trickled through of an approaching new British push in the north; tanks were said to be concentrating at St Pol, Casualty Clearing Stations were being erected and the Canadians were getting into line on the Kemmel front.

Towards the end of July, the Commander-in-Chief paid an apparently light-hearted visit to the Somme under the cloak of a Divisional Race Meeting, where he appeared to be far more interested in the horses than in the many high-ranking officers who accompanied him. The racing was not of a very high standard but Haig, perhaps remembering the 18th Division's battle record, seemed gently tolerant of an infantry style of horsemanship. I recall seeing him grinning at me when I came an almighty purler at the fourth jump in the divisional steeplechase and lay there for an interminable moment waiting for the thundering herd to place a hoof on a tender spot in my corpse.

But there were other things in his mind, and on 3rd August the general plan for the attack a week later was communicated to specially selected officers. Never had we participated in an operation kept so secret. There were less than five days in which to get all the guns and ammunition forward: as no earth was allowed to be disturbed, the thousands of rounds for the barrage had to be taken up in darkness and stacked and hidden beneath hedges, under banks and in the uncut cornfields. The guns themselves were not to be moved up until the night of the 7th; the wheels of the ammunition waggons were lapped with rope and straw was laid along metalled roads, as it once was in England outside houses where the seriously ill were lying.

It was nervy work for the Germans were very much on the alert. On 6th August, to our dismay, they made a swift, violent attack which penetrated well behind our front line. It seemed almost certain that they must have detected our preparations; however there was little to be done at this late stage and plans went on as before.

Only on one other occasion, before the battle of Poelcapelle do I remember experiencing the presentiment of impending death. Perhaps it was simply trepidation or, put more bluntly, the element of fear contributed to by the ominous geography and atmosphere of that long whale-backed promontory of high land along which we had to advance. There were few more anxious Zero Hours of waiting and watching the minute and the second hands of one's wrist watch than during the early morning of August 8th, 1918, huddled in shallow trenches astride the Bray-Corbie road, expecting at any moment a vicious enemy artillery barrage as prelude to the sudden attacks they would launch each morning. Miraculously, as we subsequently discovered in the German batteries themselves, their authorities had decided to forego their offensive habits for that morning. So at 4:20 am, when the guns supporting the main Fourth Army attack on an eleven mile front south of the Somme burst into a tornado of flame and sound, we lit our cigarettes with a sense of relief and rose up into a tussle with the German 7th Division in their forward trenches. They also seemed to have been very much on the alert. It cost us nearly 200 men before we were able to make progress and reach the final objective some two thousand yards beyond. By this time there was much confusion in a thinning early-morning fog which partly protected and partly hindered the advance.

A couple of tanks came lumbering up to cover our flank; however, unable in the mist to distinguish friend from foe, they severely wounded my poor runner and nearly did the same to me. The tanks rumbled on impervious and unfortunately disappeared by the time we had reached our objective, where we could have made best use of them. So, stumbling forward in the fog, reduced one by one to under a hundred men, we found at last the remnants of the old brickyard which were to form the left flank of our final position. A few yards away, so skilfully hidden that we had not detected them on the aerial photographs, were two batteries of field guns with their muzzles pointing towards us. The surprise was complete both to the straggling remnants of my battalion and to the German gunners who, thinking that the morning's performance was just a local raid, had settled down to breakfast under the netting over the guns.

When a whole lot of Tommies, bayonets fixed, tumbled in on top of them as they filled their mess cans, the Germans were as disconcerted as we were. Given our depleted numbers, what were we to do with an almost equal number of prisoners a mile and a half from the nearest British forces? Two of the gunners, more demoralised than the rest, provided the answer. They took their boots off and offered them to me. (In light of the numbers of discarded Egyptian boots which strewed Sinai in 1967, apparently this is a universal and time-honoured gesture of submission.) In this instance it served the situation splendidly: a couple of gunless and bootless German battery crews, escorted by a lightly wounded private, made their slow pedestrian way to the POW cages.

We were right on the line of the objectives which had been met, but Gressaire Wood, assigned equally to the Essex and

Royal Berkshires, was still some hundred yards away on the right. Meanwhile, a curious calm had descended upon the battlefield. Overhead the sun was breaking through the mists and I could hear a lark singing. The guns were muttering away south of the Somme where the Canadians and Australians had made a striking success. Above, a few of our heavy shells were still winging on their way; but otherwise all sounds had ceased. We seemed to be in an unpeopled land, unheeded by anyone.

Urgent messages were sent back recording the triumph and asking for reinforcements to further exploit the situation. Alas! Reserves are never available when they are needed and the situation in Gressaire Wood was becoming disturbing.

Not long after the captured gunners had been despatched to the rear, I was contemplating reconnoitring forward to the edge of the wood, when a large, rotund German major, resplendent with Iron Cross, emerged from the bushes and strolled across to inspect his batteries. Evidently his headquarters were there and in the fog he had failed to observe that the circumstances had changed. There was no great difficulty in demonstrating this fact to him, but it took all my halting German to explain that he could not return to the wood and that he had to join the rest of his command as a prisoner. The incident had not gone unobserved from the wood and soon we were subjected to fire from along its edges. At this juncture my adjutant returned to report that he had been unable to establish touch with any British units within a mile and it was clear that we were out in the blue entirely on our own. Machine-guns began to dribble round and gall us with their fire. Even more disheartening, our own shells were now falling around us. We seemed to be abandoned by the world.

After a couple of hours of these conditions an order arrived from Brigade to withdraw. So we smashed the breech blocks of the guns and, maintaining what covering fire we could, made the best of a scattered withdrawal under the harassing fire from some fresh guns which the enemy had aligned on the road. It was an inglorious ending to it all. My adjutant was wounded and tottered the last few hundred yards to safety on my shoulder, and many others were knocked out before finally we reached the friendly lines from which we had started out up the road to Bray: five officers and a hundred other ranks, now reduced to two officers and fifteen others.[1]

Disappointing as this was, the fortunes of war are a medley of many experiences. The distractions of our struggles on the ridges north of the Somme had assisted the flank of the main thrust along the southern bank, where an advance of six miles was made and 13,000 prisoners taken. The Hundred Days of 1918, which were to end the war at last, had been successfully begun. The high ground we had been obliged to relinquish was now of all the greater value by reason of the phenomenal gains of ground south of the Somme. So, on the evening of the 9th August, the reinforcements we had prayed for so hard made their arrival in the form of the 33rd Division of the United States Army. These fresh troops (from Manhattan, I believe) had little difficulty in sweeping over the ground that had caused us so much trouble. By the 10th August, after the German reserves in Gressaire Wood had withdrawn, the Americans were in possession of the whole of the wood. At this moment as Colonel Pritchard-Taylor of our RAMC was making sure that all the casualties had been picked up, he found that the Americans, in the comparative inexperience of their first action, were taking up position on the other side of the wood at the foot of a hill which commanded the important Bray Valley beyond. All was quiet and there was no knowledge of how far the Germans had withdrawn.

It was of obvious importance that this hill top, with its magnificent view across the town of Bray and the many features

---

1   The events described in the above paragraphs earned DB the Distinguished Service Order. The citation reads: 'For conspicuous gallantry and good leadership. He led his battalion some 5,000 yards through thick fog and against heavy opposition to the final objective, withdrawing most skilfully to the first objective when almost surrounded by the enemy, and consolidating it. Two days later, when adjacent troops were finding difficulties in consolidating their positions, he personally led their outposts some 400 yards forward and under heavy fire supervised consolidation. Throughout he set a fine example of cool courage to all ranks.' (*Supplement to the Edinburgh Gazette*, Oct 17, 1918, p.3775).

of the Somme, should be in our hands. So when Pritchard-Taylor drew up in his ambulance at Brigade HQ where I was resting after the strenuous events of August 8th, it did not take long for me to climb in beside him and go forward to the area I had grown to know so well.

Patrolling circumspectly to the top of the hill, we found as expected that it was unoccupied, but at the foot of the slope on the other side a party of grey-uniformed troops had similar ideas and were making their way rapidly to the vantage point where we were. My companion volunteered to do his best to divert the enemy while I doubled back to the Americans to persuade them to come forward. It was touch and go: by the time I had explained the situation and got the GIs on the move to the crest, the Germans were off-limbered and opening fire on the ubiquitous RAMC Colonel who was trying to simulate an army by rapid appearances at many points. The Americans won by a short head and swung their guns rapidly into action from a small natural redoubt that formed the crest of the hill,

'Pleased to meet you, but do you guys usually go about doing this?' said the American Major as he bade us a grateful farewell.

'Glad to see you. It's just a part of the Allied service,' we replied, as we wished them luck and set off back to Brigade HQ to report a very satisfactory outcome to the arrival of those belated reinforcements.

10th Essex Regiment, 1918
Lieut-Colonel T M Banks MC DSO in centre of front row

6

LA GUERRE FINIE

The days after these hectic events were also not devoid of drama. It transpired that the holdup on the right of the objective line on the 8th of August was due to heavy casualties in the Berkshires, including their Commanding Officer, Colonel N B Hudson, in later days after the war, the Bishop of Newcastle, who was hit in five places by close-range fire and had to be evacuated during the fight.

The 8th Royal Berkshires were now without a commanding officer. As my predecessor in the Essex returned after a spell of sick leave, I was posted to replace Colonel Hudson and found myself wearing the Berkshire dragon for most of the rest of the war. It was a poignant moment when I bade farewell to my old Essex comrades, drawn up in a hollow square on the ground of one of the battlefields of the Somme where they had made so notable a contribution. We had embarked for France three years before a thousand strong; out of that number there were now comparatively few left. Only one officer remained other than myself. We used cheerfully to comment to each other that the finger of fate was turning ominously in our direction. So perhaps the time for a change had come.

Two exciting actions marked my somewhat anomalous progress through the next two months. In one case, after the division had swept through Albert, I had the strange task of clearing Trones Wood which we had done once before from a different direction during the early days of the Somme Offensive in 1916.

As we made our way cautiously up Caterpillar Valley, from which I had been carried down on July 2nd 1916, it was all very different – deserted and desolate and as quiet as the grave until we rounded the corner where the German artillery dug-outs originally yielded an exotic medley of loot. But as soon as we came into view of Trones Wood there was a fusillade of fire.

My mixed force of the 8th Royal Berks, two companies of the 10th Essex, two 18-pounders and a mortar battery, had to be manoeuvred into position and a barrage worked out. After a long day of acute tension (including a counterattack by the Francis Joseph's Prussian Guards), we launched an evening attack and the Berks and Essex went through the German Guards with bayonets, killing over fifty of the enemy and capturing seventy. This was my only experience of a mixed command in action and very proud of it I was.

By now it was the end of August. Some twenty days of the Hundred had elapsed and we were biting well into the open country so far as, in its devastation, it could be called 'open'. For the first time it was possible to manoeuvre and many casualties were saved by skilful turning movements.

There were some strange episodes. As we advanced through St Pierre Vaast Wood a German staff car came racketting down a shell-pocked drive with Staff Captain Nutcombe Hume (after the war, Sir Nutcombe Hume of Charterhouse in the City of London). By a bold take-over move (*not* within the code!) he had managed to appropriate this from his opposite numbers and so make a marked improvement in the mobility of the Brigade Staff at a vital stage in the operations. Mobility, too, brought unwonted problems for the gunners who were now boldly advancing their batteries and single sniping guns into the forefront of the battle wherever it raged. Water for their horses in this ravaged land was non-existent and the Royal Engineers came to the rescue by sinking windlass wells. Thus, in one way and another, we experienced the exhilaration of open fighting: gaining one day a ruined village or, another night, a devastated sugar beet factory – looking like some space-fiction fantasy, with its demented twisted pipes and tumbled reservoirs, blown up by the enemy in their hasty retreat.

Eventually the outposts of the Hindenburg Line near the St Quentin Canal were reached. Here it was evident from the stiffening resistance that the much-vaunted last ditch was going to be strenuously defended. Yak, Zebra, Duncan, Doleful and Egg Posts and Tombois Farm – a sombre catalogue of sinister fights – each called for separate subjugation and claimed their toll of victims. It was in one of these that we lost our faithful Major J C Parke, the famous Wimbledon Tennis player and Rugby Cap, who had endeared himself to all and been in the thick of the action since he joined the 10th Essex in March 1918.

The big fight for the main Hindenburg Line fell principally to the 27th American Division. The Line here was at its strongest as it included the Canal du Nord, itself a formidable obstacle. There was also the notorious Bellicourt Tunnel, reputed to have been used by the blockaded Germans as a front-line 'factory' for the ghastly purpose of making explosives by rendering down fat from the corpses from the Somme battlefields.

It is pathetic to recall the heavy slaughter incurred here by the comparatively inexperienced US troops. At this particular place for some reason the American dead were buried where they fell. I remember the thick tragic swathe of wooden crosses which sloped up the knoll leading to the main works of the Hindenburg Line where over 5,000 had been killed. At one machine-gun point, after the battle, was found a pencilled note by a German officer:-

> Dear Tommy,
> From this place I shot 60 American soldiers;
> They came like sheeps.

The barrage had failed lamentably and we all honoured the superb bravery with which these unpractised troops stormed this formidable feature and, breaking through, opened the way for the Allies into the untouched country beyond.

By the middle of October 1918 we were on the move into this long-promised land, peopled by wan, scarified French folk who for four years had known the severity of the invader's yoke. They gathered in groups around the men in khaki who had brought them deliverance, trying to communicate the gratitude which showed in their eyes. Men went out of their way to doff their caps to our officers, proud and happy to do it to their liberators, where before only the jackboot and the whip secured compliance with the German orders.

They told us tales of severe treatment of British prisoners, of secret food smuggled through to them by the peasants and the rigorous punishments that followed discovery; tales of deportation of French inhabitants, of heavy fines for trumped-up misdemeanours, stories of hopes raised in 1916 and 1917 when the sound of the Allied guns crept eastward in the Somme and Cambrai battles and of bitter disappointment when the advance was stemmed, and in the Spring of 1918, the Allied front was rolled back again.

The immediate fighting now developed into one vast rear guard action as the Germans resisted stubbornly at every vantage point. But though resistance remained, there were signs that the enemy's morale was weakening.

In Le Cateau we were greeted by an astonishing display of French *tricouleurs* which evidently had been secretly preserved in hope of the day of liberation. In two woodland villages the cellars in which the Germans had taken shelter could not be bombed as they were also sheltering many inhabitants. The Divisional Staff, with their red insignia, were often able to bring reassurance to the inhabitants more readily than the fighting troops; they frequently would come up to the front of the advance for this purpose. For example, Capt Cullum Welch GSO3 was able to do some notable work in a new and particularly resplendent red-tabbed tunic which had arrived opportunely. How much more effective, indeed, might have been the regalia that he wore when he became Lord Mayor of London in 1956!

For the people of Hecq, perhaps, as great a thrill as any was the sight of a highlander in the kilt; all the women and children in the place crept from their lairs to stare and grin at this strange phenomenon.

We were now on the verge of the Mormal Forest, at the end of the Hundred Days and very near the Armistice. Almost unperceived in the front fighting line, where newspapers were rarities and radio broadcast news of course as yet unknown, the end of the war was reached. Unlike the frenzied scenes in London and other big cities, the cessation of hostilities was marked by a solemnity and a quiet thankfulness in which, I think it is true to say, there was a deep and genuine memory of comrades who had not lived to celebrate the cause that had bound us all together.

It is that sense of common risk and endeavour – so rare in peacetime – that is the background of the November Remembrance ceremonies. How long they can survive the passage of time is much open to question.

The 18th Division consisted entirely of 'three years or the duration' men;[1] therefore it was decided that they should be demobilised early and not proceed to the Rhine. So we settled down more or less where we were to await the golden moment that would see us become civilians again.

At first the official enthusiasm was for salvage operations, which kept units on the fringes of the battle-wilderness for the purposes of gathering up the rusty aftermath of war. Miles and miles of barbed wire were reeled in, hundreds and hundreds of tin hats – the comparatively unflattering British type and the more sinister German – were picked up, as well as bombs, rifles, shells, guns, ammunition boxes, derelict wagons and every form of war material: all accumulated in mountainous heaps along the sides of the roads. The energy expended on the new task in the first weeks was immense and I have often wondered what happened to it all as the machinery for removing it was quite inadequate. At best it seemed a poor job and a little ironic that the victorious army should have to scavenge the dirty mess left by the defeated.

So we turned our interest to other things and the official emphasis on salvage was switched to education, as a preparation for return to civil life and occupations. This, in wintry weather conditions amidst the dreariness of the old battlefields seemed a much better bet: anyone, irrespective of rank, who had any experience as a teacher was roped in to extemporise this strangest of do-it-yourself universities.

A large barn with a shell-punctured roof served for the class

---

1   A reference to the terms of enlistment for volunteers into Kitchener's Army – men were invited to enlist 'for three years, or for the duration of the war' (https://wordhistories.net/2017/10/23/for-the-duration-origin/).

rooms. Here a small cadre of us, armed with such books and pamphlets as were sent out from England, sought to instruct our eager proselytes in a haphazard medley of subjects, dictated by the Ministry of Reconstruction such as Shorthand, Political Economy, Agriculture, Music, Steam-Engines and Art. We found one or two men who were completely illiterate; the delight of one boy who told me that he had managed to write his first letter home to his mother was very touching.

Christmas intervened while we were still scantily housed in these devastated parts. The financial authorities were wise enough to loosen the purse strings and our transport roamed to the gates of Paris to stock up for the festivities. Nor did we forget the local inhabitants, who had crept back to their shattered homes. The Quartermaster excelled himself in devising little Christmas gifts for them out of our ration supplies: perhaps the most popular were the cakes of soap wrapped up in the familiar brown toilet paper of the trenches!

Early in January the first drafts left for demobilisation in England. This was a time of some tension as the Government had adopted an unpopular scheme of priorities which, with the fear of unemployment for those chosen to return home last, caused much disquiet in the ranks – even some mutinies at Calais. The thing to do was to keep everyone as fully occupied as possible, so it was a relief when orders came to move to a more hospitable district and take up quarters in the little town of Clary.

Clary was typical of the small farm-cum-factory townships in the north of France. The inhabitants combined the tilling of the fields with working their looms and lived in substantially built houses. In 1914, the invasion and the battle of Le Cateau burst like a thunder-clap upon the quiet, industrious routine of their lives. Flushed with visions of easy victory before the fall of the leaves, the Prussians broke into the little town one September night and for two days terror reigned. The town hall was burnt down and the glare of many other fires lit the skies.

Shots rang out around the street corners. Cafés were sacked. Up the road, within a few hundred yards of the village, a

Company of the Royal Dublin Fusiliers, surrounded in an old distillery, fought a long fight until half of them were killed and the remnant surrendered for lack of ammunition. No wonder that the townsfolk of Clary spoke with shudders of those nightmare times of 1914.

The wave of ferocity passed and the long years of occupation followed. Hard years they were, growing harder as the pinch of famine became more severe. The youngsters grew prematurely aged; one could see it in their lustreless eyes. The old people carried on. Then when the British brought deliverance, they seemed to say their *Nunc Dimittis* and passed peacefully away. It was remarkable to learn the number of old folk who died during this winter of victory.

Thus was Clary when we marched up the main street, the faithful Essex village band heading us bravely and the pavements lined with welcoming citizens. It was a paradise after the wastes we had quitted and we revelled in the good billets and the warm welcome, and set about organising all the gaiety possible. One of the big features was the opening of a large canteen in a reconstructed hut, rather like the NAAFI of future days. Tokens were issued in the form of cyclostyled paper currency to the troops and their benefactors: most popular but possibly illegal. Cinema performances were free for the children, to whom movies were a novel experience; indeed all ages reacted with exuberant enthusiasm. The dances organised for the men and young women were red letter events in the lives of soldiers and civilians alike. These brought down the fulminations of the *curé* and in response I received a petition from '*les jeunes filles patriotes de Clary*', begging to continue the dancing.

Here was a pretty problem which I took to M le Maire. He shrugged his shoulders. '*Que voulez-vous, M le Colonel?*' Curés were like that and young folk are young only once. And as the French Constitution has a blind eye in matters ecclesiastical: '*Alors, continuez les danses, M'sieur.*' So the dancing continued with renewed vigour and, as far as I could judge, kept relationships more open and satisfactory than they might otherwise have been.

Après la Guerre finie,
Et les Anglais partis,
Mademoiselle in the family way,
Après la Guerre finie.

the *gamins* used to sing. But I don't think that the birth-rate increased abnormally in Clary.

Gradually successive demobilisation drafts reduced us to no more than the skeleton of a battalion. It was something of an ordeal to pass down the departing ranks, shaking each of these gallant old comrades by the hand, thanking them for all they had done and wishing them luck in their new lives. We issued each one with a scroll of achievement and an address to write to if they needed help. But it seemed an anti-climax to finish up with no more than that, and the place grew lonelier as the parties moved out of the gates to the tunes of the regimental march, the Yankee march 'Over There' (curiously enough!) and the final strains of 'Auld Lang Syne'.

By June 1919 we were down to cadre strength and the time had come when transport was at last available to take us back to England. There were only a score or so of us left: a rudimentary colour party and two officers – the Quartermaster and myself. The band had gone, the Officers' Mess had dwindled to a café table; almost shamefacedly we marched out down the street. But the word had gone round that we were going. The last chapter of the war was ending for both Clary and ourselves. They wanted to recognise it. So from house after house they emerged, waving, clapping and blowing kisses. The *jeunes filles patriotes* went further and ran up to us to bestow them. One little *demoiselle*, with whom I had danced once or twice, came to the front and linked her arm with mine – to the romantic joy of the populace. M le Maire appeared in the sash and appurtenances of his office; and even the *curé* came to the door of his church to wave us an indulgent *adieu*.

So, down the long road where the Old Contemptibles had marched four and a half years before, we made our diminished way, while the waving figures grew smaller and smaller in the distance: back across the Channel to Blighty and back to Salisbury Plain.

The *London Evening News* gave us our epitaph:

Essex Battalion's Sombre Homecoming

Over the holiday season (Whitsun. 1919) there was quietly disbanded in a tucked away part of Wiltshire a gallant battalion, the 10th Essex, which was born in the feverish days of the autumn of 1914, formed part of what was colloquially known as Kitchener's Second Hundred Thousand, and saw the war through on some of the bloodiest fields of France.

No glitter, no electric cheering ceremony accompanied the disbandment. The Colours were sent quietly to the Depot at Warley, and the men dispersed to their own homes.

The official figures show the fighting qualities of the Battalion :-

Passed through the Battalion (Officers)............227
(Men)...............5,274
Total killed or died of wounds.........................1,103

One in five who served with the unit, even for a few days, was killed. And I had been with them throughout. Not very good odds of survival!

But, *Dei Gratia*, at the end of the 'duration', I came back alive and intact to the somnolent suburbs of London on a Whitsun Bank Holiday, stripped of glory, danger and excitement. The next day, I donned a bowler hat to attend the seemingly even more somnolent headquarters of the General Post Office.

GPO North, St Martin's le Grand, 1935
(POST 118/291, © Royal Mail Group Ltd 2020
courtesy of the Postal Museum)

7

THE GENERAL POST OFFICE

The heart and centre of that great mixed bag of communications and financial activities – the General Post Office – is sited in the City of London around St Martin's le Grand, just north of St Paul's Cathedral.

Its long genesis from the days of the Tudor Monarchs – when the Royal Mail was organised to facilitate the Crown's supervision of communication between recalcitrant elements – through the institution of mounted post boys and posting establishments, until the mail coaches took their place and, ultimately, the railways paved the way to the great revolution of Rowland Hill's Universal Penny Post in 1840: all these activities had stamped the Post Office with the premier characteristics of mail-carrying; and the Bull and Mouth Inn in the City, whence the mail coaches regularly departed, became the natural centre for the postal services.

Onto this was grafted the Central Telegraph Office when the technological developments of the 19th century added this speedier method of communication to the resources of the Department. In 1861, when Gladstone added the Post Office Savings Bank, space for expansion was already very restricted and the Savings Bank Headquarters was moved later from the City to Kensington. With the acquisition of the National Telephone Company in 1911 it was almost literally a case of there being no room in the inn: in spite of its importance, Telephone Headquarters (together with its ancillary engineering activities) have usually been housed in scattered peripheral accommodation. Indeed, it is noteworthy that the nearest operative telephone exchanges lay away from GPO Headquarters to the south of St Paul's.

All this, understandably, left a new arrival in 1919 a good deal baffled and bewildered. The large Victorian building known as GPO North, looking like a very solid chunk of Whitehall transplanted in the City and a monument of wasted space and land in those golden acres, housed the Secretary's Office, the Comptroller and Accountant General and, in a grudging corner, the five rooms allotted to the Postmaster General and his assistant.

Across a bridge lay GPO South, which was a busy hive of telegraph machines and operators. Further to the west, beyond a statue of Rowland Hill which seemed to eye with constant reproach his successors who abandoned the Penny Post, stood the large modern buildings of the London Postal Service.

The Engineer-in-Chief's staff, vital as it is to the telecommunications side, curiously enough was nowhere evident. Indeed, it was years before I managed to locate it all in the variegated adjoining offices. The whole effect was one of random incoherence; like Topsy it had 'just growed' and like Topsy, I suppose, it did not quite know why.[1]

As a government department, the General Post Office had naturally taken on the standard Treasury outlook of the 19th Century and much of the Gladstonian tradition in finance. There was always lurking in the political background a wary fear that the Chancellor of the Exchequer would seek to use the Posts as a means of raising revenue. This finally disappeared by the time Edward VIII came to the throne (in 1936) and I can remember a certain degree of gratification when the word 'Revenue', was finally omitted from the postage stamp at that time.

The guiding principle was to make ends meet, to balance income and expenditure with as little of the latter as possible. This was long before the modern days of cost-effectiveness; indeed, cost accountancy was in its infancy. It would be perhaps untrue to say that on the postal side there was no ultimate objective. To make a daily delivery of letters to every household in the land was no mean object; and to do that within the

---

1   A reference to a character in the novel Uncle Tom's Cabin (1851-52) by Harriet Beecher Stowe. When Topsy is asked whether she knows who made her (that is, whether she has heard of God), she replies 'I expect I grow'd'. Something that 'just grew, like Topsy' implies that it has become very large in an unplanned way.

compass of a penny charge, as Roland Hill had planned, was so outstanding an achievement that it seemed as if the postal authorities could have little to aim at beyond adapting and perfecting this objective. The telegraph, when it arrived in the 1870s, was grafted onto the postal structure; but the telephones at the end of the century grew up almost entirely independently.

Good postal organisation depends upon rapid and economical transportation, and involves a high degree of manual work in sorting and delivery. Developments in transport, therefore, had a profound influence upon the posts. As well, the large labour content of the work has led to the build-up of a massive force of postmen and indoor staff, with a corresponding need for effective handling of the morale of the service. First-class pension schemes and medical attention formed an important part in cultivating this *esprit de corps*. In those days, when recruitment into the outdoor staff came mainly from the armed forces, this was a noteworthy feature of the Post Office.

These matters were handled by the Staff Branch, to which I found myself assigned to deal with sickness and superannuation. All the many ills to which the flesh is heir exhibited themselves in a flood of paper cases which flowed across my desk. As time went on, they began to transform me into a chronic hypochondriac. It was terribly impersonal too – all on paper with little that one could do beyond referring the problematic medical cases to the Chief Medical Officer, Doctor Sinclair. He was a sagacious and lovable Scottish medico who exercised his sway from a small room in GPO South, from which he controlled the many local Post Office doctors throughout the United Kingdom; he saw the particularly difficult cases himself when necessary, or referred them to specialists. It was a first-rate National Health Service long in advance of the nationwide facilities which came in later. As even a small cog in a large wheel which revolved steadily and successfully in promoting the health and welfare of nearly a quarter of a million employees, I suppose that I should have been satisfied. The personal contribution, however, was ludicrously routine and small: files of paper on a desk were a poor substitute for the livelier files of infantrymen it had been my lot to deal with in the less humdrum conditions of the preceding four years.

The walls of the little grey room I occupied, half-cleaned to shoulder-height by Mrs Mopp[2] with the remaining space left to the mercies of the Office of Works – a typical Civil Service compromise – seemed to close in and crush me until I could stand the claustrophobic atmosphere no longer. I applied for transfer to the Ministry of Labour who were advertising some area supervisor appointments which looked as if they might take one a bit closer to the wide open spaces and the new dawn of National Reconstruction offered in the promises of 'a land fit for heroes'.[3]

The placid surfaces of the Staff Branch then began to stir. Apparently my war record, with DSO, MC, *Croix de Guerre* and Mentions had attracted more interest in the upper strata of the administration than I had realised. I was sent for by one senior officer after another until I reached the august presence of the Secretary himself, Sir Evelyn Murray.

Sir Evelyn was a typical product of Eton and Christchurch and had swum rapidly through the university entrance at the Board of Education to the secretaryship of the Post Office. In those days the definition of the Secretary's duties was vague, as indeed it has been ever since Rowland Hill set the seal of distinction upon it until the present century, when successive generations have sought the elusive solution to the crucial problem of socialism and nationalised industry: how to find the *via media* between public and political interest and enterprising and efficient execution.

2   A reference to a character in a popular radio comedy show called ITMA that ran on BBC radio from 1939-1949. Mrs. Mopp was a char lady who became famous for always asking 'Can I do yer now, Sir?'
3   In August 1917 the Lloyd George government created the Ministry of Reconstruction with the promise of creating a 'land fit for heroes'. It set up a plethora of committees that investigated many aspects of life in Britain, ranging from housing and local government to labour relations and the post-war economy. The reality was major industrial chaos and disruptive strikes. It ended in disappointment – when unemployment rose rapidly during the 1921 economic slump, the Ministry was shelved, leaving many of its promises unfulfilled.

To Murray and the old Civil Service School the answer was that the ministerial function was to set the policy and the objectives, and the executive function was to steer the machine towards those ends. It was as simple as that, and those were the principles which governed Murray's long regime of twenty years at St Martin's le Grand. In subsequent times we were to attempt a synthesis between the two functions – rather akin in some respects to the relationship in commercial concerns between the Chairman of the Board and the Managing Director. But that was still to come.

Murray received me sympathetically and counselled me strongly to forget the idea of the Ministry of Labour. The Post Office offered me good opportunities and, 'You never know what waits around the corner.' Sure enough, within a few weeks I found myself moved from the cramped conditions of the Sick Leave Duty to the ample room next door to Sir Evelyn's own office, and earning a further one hundred and fifty pounds a year as Private Secretary to the Secretary.

It was not a lot of money when it all added up – with the proceeds of my War Gratuity, about £500 a year – but it enabled me to get married and take a tiny flat in Bayswater, of which we were inordinately proud.[4] We used the snob address of Hyde Park, W2; but our ruder friends insisted that it was Paddington, until I appealed to the London Postal Controller himself who ruled in favour of Hyde Park.

There were advantages in being at the Post Office after all!

---

4   DB married Dorothy, daughter of Norman Webster of *Roseneath*, The Grange, Guernsey on 7 June 1921 in Woking (pictured right in 1936).

It was a great change in many ways. Instead of the drab journey from the northern heights, with the funny little Great Northern tank engines puffing along the heavily populated slopes of Stroud Green and Crouch End, I started the day, as I long continued to do, with a good walk through Hyde Park: a strangely unpopulated oasis in the midst of the humming traffic all around, where it was rare at that time in the morning to meet any live beings other than the occasional horse and rider, or the grey squirrels which would clamber up one's arms to coax a piece of biscuit. Riding on the Central Line on the Tube I often found myself sitting next to Sir Montague Norman, the Governor of the Bank of England; an idiosyncratic bearded figure with his railway ticket stuck in the ribbon of his hat, who apparently kept much the same hours at the bank as we did at the GPO.

Arrived at St Martin's le Grand, there was an entirely different range and variety of duties to perform. The first thing was to arrange the Secretary's papers and appointments and, strangely enough, even to test that the telephones were working! There had been one cataclysmic day when all his phones were out of order; thenceforth it was a must to see that for at least one telephone in the City of London there was no interruption of the service.

In many of the older government offices there is a device, peculiar as far as I know to the Civil Service, of a small closable peep-hole through the door leading from the Private Secretary's room into the chieftain's lair. Thus, an inconspicuous observation could be kept upon the great man's visitors and the progress of the affairs with which he was dealing. It was a simple but efficacious way of keeping the public service moving and avoiding awkward interruptions to its performance. I did not, however, realise at first that it cut both ways: on one occasion when I wanted some parliamentary questions dealt with urgently, I peered through the peep-hole and found an eye peeping through at me from the other side. Both parties were simultaneously embarrassed and no reference was subsequently made to the incident, so I did not discover whether it was merely curiosity on Murray's part, or whether, in fact, he wanted to satisfy himself that I was actually working.

There was a notable morning when his telephones went out of order and I had hastily to summon aid from the London Telephone Service who sent a dungaree-clad engineer with all speed to inspect the instruments on his desk. Then, to my horror, I heard Murray arrive; hastening to the peep-hole, I saw him stride across the room, deposit his top hat on its usual side table and begin to circulate around his desk and the dungareed attendant. Apparently he said nothing and the engineer went on with his work until, with a sudden inspiration, Murray darted to his desk and rang my bell. 'Banks,' he said when I entered. 'You might tell that man to go away.' Fortunately, the technical work had been virtually completed and smooth working was soon restored all round. But for long afterwards I was careful to arrive at the office early enough to get the ritual telephone test completed within an ample margin of time.

Policy action at the GPO originates in the time-honoured procedure of the 'PMG's Minute', which is a submission in a vertically truncated form of a proposal from the administration to the minister; the large margin filling half the page is presumably intended to enable the PMG to express himself with equal volubility, although I never remember a PMG ever putting more than a few words at the end – after which the appropriate action was initiated and the document became a historic record to be preserved in perpetuity.

When the Post Office is under general public or political criticism, which happens with almost cyclical regularity every seven years or so, the minutes are frequent and largely self-originating. At other times, apart from certain routine reviews, the initiative depends upon the personalities of the minister and of the Secretary. At this particular time in the early 1920s the Postmaster General, Mr A H Illingworth, was suffering from high blood pressure and disinclined to initiate any drastic policy. The field was clear, therefore, for a thorough review of telephone charges, and an extensive and probably unique process of costing all the factors involved. It was a fundamental work and, although it was handicapped by the fact that automatic telephone equipment was still immature, it formed the basis on which the British telephone tariffs have been constructed ever since. Perhaps it could be argued that the approach was, too rigid, with little or no allowance for commercial considerations or customer appeal. That was to come under the Kingsley Wood regime in the thirties. But with sound prescience Murray provided that, as far as foreseeable, a reasonable margin of profit was loaded on to the main volume of ordinary calls. It was only when this principle was neglected that the telephones began to head for financial trouble.

There was no lack in the variety of matters to be dealt with. Parliamentary questions, as in all government departments, claimed a large part of the morning's work. Since the minister was due to appear in person before the Westminster footlights that afternoon, it was natural that he took a close and urgent interest in making the best possible preparations. This was reflected all the way down the line, including the remoter offices, in the remarkable loyalty and identity of purpose with which everyone concerned seemed to be determined to get the better of potential interrogators. Of course there was an element of self-interest as well as team-spirit in this attitude, but it can be recorded that, whatever the temptations to score points, it was a sacred and inviolable rule that the strict truth must be told. Very rarely have I known a minister try to evade this rigid code; even if he did envisage the possibility, the rhadamanthine rectitude of Civil Service Standards invariably prevailed.

The annual estimates presented to the House of Commons were always a testing time for Postmasters General. Apart from the general airing of grievances they afforded, the minister had to be prepared for local questions from all quarters of the house from members anxious to earn a good mention in their constituencies. So, the officials concerned mustered as strongly as space permitted in the cramped obscurity of the official gallery behind the speaker's chair, prepared to relay any and every form of information to the front bench through the Parliamentary Private Secretary, who spent the evening worming his way across the back benches as inconspicuously as possible.

A parliamentary stroke of strategy which caused much chortling occurred when the opposition had been lambasting the inefficiency of the telephones and maintaining that the only way to make them function properly was to put them under private enterprise. The PMG looked appealingly back to the official gallery and Murray quickly produced and marked a back copy of Hansard which read somewhat as follows:

> It is scandalous how inefficient this important adjunct of social intercourse and business enterprise has become. Not only is it virtually impossible to secure speedy connections or obtain satisfactory service, but the charges levied are out of all reason.

The PMG looked quickly at the Hansard, outside and in, and when the time came to reply, the minister in charge quoted the passage to the loud and vociferous endorsement of the opposition. 'And that,' he then finished, 'is the view of Honourable Members opposite in 1910, when the telephones were under the commercial administration of the National Telephone Company!'

So passed a couple of interesting years, invaluable for the future as an experience of the exercise of the higher administrative qualities – both how, and sometimes how not to do things. Remembering the incident of the telephone engineer, it was easy to perceive that the leadership was unduly remote and lacking in the personal touch. To some extent this is inevitable in so large an organisation where the dichotomy between the political and the executive function in an operative government department tends to be divisive. It can probably be better avoided in a corporation structure – like the model which the Post Office is now adopting.[5]

From the vantage-point of Private Secretary I could see that the relationship between Secretary and PMG was often

---

5   Writing in the 1960s, DB was referring to the structural changes brought about by Harold Wilson's government which resulted in the Post Office Act 1969.

From "The Evening News"
TRAMP, TRAMP, TRAMP, THE BOYS ARE MARCHING

It is felt that the constant changes in the office of Postmaster-General are not conducive to the better working of the department

The Tatler, 6 June 1923

not as easy as might be desired, particularly as the ministerial changes at this period were so frequent. Indeed they inspired a newspaper cartoon of five PMGs in rapid succession headed 'Tramp, Tramp, Tramp, the boys are marching'.

Part of the Private Secretary's duties was to keep things running as smoothly as possible; so when my opposite number with the PMG was transferred to the Home Office, I was accordingly promoted to his post with an increment of £50 a year and a new and fascinating series of experiences.

The first of my new Chiefs was F G Kellaway (Liberal MP for Bedford), an able politician who had just missed selection for higher office. Unusually for most of the Postmasters General appointed in my time, he had a genuine primary interest in the Post Office and its affairs. He was the first to set up an internal board, a feature continued in the political history of the department since then; even more more significantly, he created an advisory council of prominent businessmen. Among these were the chairman of Bovril and a leading banker who was quite enthralled by our problems. I spent an eye-opening weekend at his large estate in Gloucestershire, seeking desperately to conceal from an overwhelming butler that I had travelled third class on the railway to get there.

An even more notable member was Gordon Selfridge[6], who was completely convinced that a return to the Penny Post was essential but much baffled as to how to achieve it. He used to address long hortatory letters on this subject, both to Kellaway and Murray, and send carbon copies to all the members of the council. Turnover and advertising were the two means which he thought would achieve his objective; he wanted to advertise on every telegraph post and on the back of postage stamps, specimens of which were printed for the council but which never got further than the King's stamp collection.

Most vividly I remember an invitation by Gordon Selfridge to visit him at his famous Oxford Street store.

'I don't suppose you know it.' he said.

'Most certainly, I do.' I replied. 'I always get my hair cut there'.

'Well then next time, ask the cashier to bring you upstairs to my office.'

And this I did. As a good business man, he wanted to persuade me that he was insufficiently remunerated for the Post Office which he had opened as a novel attraction in one part of the store. He called for his departmental ledgers and there under Post Office were the red ink entries which showed its unprofitability.

As he turned through the ledger I noticed that the radio department, then a novelty development, also showed up in red. So I asked him why he continued to put up with losses on that.

'It attracts customers to the paying lines' he said.

6   The American-born founder of the famous department store in Oxford Street. He remained chairman from 1909-1941.

'Can't you treat the Post Office services similarly?' I enquired. He looked rather straight at me. 'H'm, so they're not without some business sense in the Post Office,' he said. 'Come and see the shop.' He put on his shiny top hat and treated me to his famous daily *tour-de-monde,* in which he delighted to show that he knew the wholesale and selling prices of everything from bath salts to suit cases and kept himself up to the moment on the rates of turnover.

Kellaway made me secretary of both the new Post Office councils. Apparently I acquitted myself not unsatisfactorily in his eyes as he took me to lunch at the Savoy with Marconi, and the great man offered me an opening in one of his companies. It was not very precisely specified and I was by then much more firmly established in the idea of a Post Office career and not inclined to follow it up. In those days there was a faint degree of impropriety in the idea of transferring from public to private employment; other preoccupations in the form of a general election intervened. So that particular 'might-have-been' passed by.

The General Election of 1922 marked the end of the Liberal Postmasters General: their records at the Post Office, stretching back to the inauguration of the Universal Penny Post, the Post Office Savings Bank, the Telegraphs and the Telephones and the Parcel Post by the blind PMG Henry Fawcett in 1882, had always been regarded as a particularly bright feature of Liberalism.

Kellaway was succeeded by Neville Chamberlain, whose appointment arose from a complex of party considerations following the break-up of Lloyd George's coalition government.[7] Although Chamberlain was pleased to get back into office, it was apparent that he was disappointed that it was not something higher and he took comparatively little interest in departmental affairs. Indeed, much of his time at the office was absorbed by

---

7   The 1922 General Election was held on Wednesday 15 November 1922. It was the first election held after most of the Irish counties left the United Kingdom to form the Irish Free State, and was won by Andrew Bonar Law's Conservatives, who gained an overall majority over Labour, led by J R Clynes, and a divided Liberal Party.

work on the details of a project for a ship canal from the Severn to Birmingham.

After little more than six months at St Martin's le Grand, Chamberlain moved on to the Ministry of Health and was followed for a short time by Sir William Joynson-Hicks and then, more durably, by Sir Laming Worthington-Evans. In a bewilderingly short time I had to serve a succession of masters each with markedly different characters; and if I learnt no more from this protean procession, I certainly gathered something in adaptability.

Sir Laming Worthington-Evans, like Neville Chamberlain, had suffered some disappointments in the post-coalition reshuffles. But, on coming to the Post Office, he had been given cabinet rank and a mandate to organise a permanent structure for the new broadcasting phenomenon which was then taking shape under the vigorous leadership of Sir John Reith.[8] These were uncharted seas; but 'Worthy' was able by his robust and skillful helmsmanship to reach an agreed basis for the Royal Charter which founded the British Broadcasting Corporation in 1927. I remember well the great sense of achievement and relief with which the final lines were settled on a tennis lawn at his country house in Surrey one fine summer's afternoon. And if Sir Laming Worthington-Evans did little more than that during his tenure of office as PMG, he earned himself a niche in the halls of history at that moment.

Like his predecessors of this period, he was marked for higher office and within a few months he left for the War Office. Before he left he told me that he thought it would be a good thing for me if I got some experience in an executive post; he had arranged with Murray for me to be appointed Deputy Controller of the Post Office Savings Bank and he was confident that it would open the way to other things.

So when 'Worthy' wended his way to Whitehall, I walked a different path across the park in the mornings and made my way to a new official existence in Blythe Road, West Kensington.

8   Sir John, later Baron Reith (1889-1971), the first Director General of the BBC.

Post Office Savings Bank, Blythe Road, West Kensington
(POST 118/248, © Royal Mail Group Ltd 2020
courtesy of the Postal Museum)

8
BLYTHE ROAD

The Post Office Savings Bank was founded by an Act of Parliament passed by Mr Gladstone in 1861. This originated from a wide philanthropic movement to encourage thrift in the working classes, who were then emerging from their poverty-stricken conditions into a measure of prosperity which was often conducive to intemperance. The local post offices henceforward became available as well as the gin-palaces as repositories for the people's spare cash at the end of the week. A virtual avalanche of deposits from all classes flooded into the national coffers.

It is estimated that one in ten of the population now has a Savings Bank account and that at least one in four people have been depositors at some time in their lives. Certainly. HM the Queen and Princess Margaret held Post Office Savings Bank books; as children they used to operate them themselves at the St James' St Post Office branch.

Initially, transactions from all over the country were notified to the Accountant General of the GPO in the City, where a vast army of clerks recorded them in individual accounts and soon absorbed all obtainable accommodation. At the end of the 19th century a huge new building in the prevailing neo-byzantine style was commissioned in the west of London and erected on the site of the famous Buffalo Bill's Circus in Blythe Road, near Olympia in West London.[1]

It was a notable bit of architecture, constructed to bear the weight of an immense number of heavy ledgers, into which thousands of individual transactions from the twenty-three thousand post offices all over the country were entered daily. The volume of paper which flowed in each morning required a

---

1   The Post Office Savings Bank remained at Blythe House until the late 1960s. In 1969 it was renamed National Savings, a separate government department under the Treasury. In 1996 it became an Executive Agency of the Chancellor of the Exchequer.

special postal sorting office to handle it; and the dozen rooms which housed the ledgers were each of the length of a normal football pitch.

By the end of the Great War the idea of mass-production in the factories had become commonplace. Here – an exception at the time – was an example *par excellence* of clerical operations on a mass-production scale, performed by a staff of five thousand people: more than half of them women. The introduction of women into the Civil Service had first taken place at the Post Office Savings Bank; coupled with the political campaign of 'Votes for Women', it led to much controversy at Blythe Road. Segregation was the principle of the time: woe betide a man who strayed into the women's sections without permission. Indeed, special measures were taken in the first days of the occupation of the new building to board up the balustrades of the staircases, lest men catch improper views of female ankles as the ladies went up and down their stairs.

Curiously enough, my appointment to the Savings Bank with a mission to overhaul and modernise it, coincided (unknown to me) with that of a new Lady Superintendent, charged – it subsequently transpired – with a similar task from a feminist angle. Fortunately, the new Lady Superintendent, Miss Curtis, later Dame Myra Curtis, Principal of Newnham College, Cambridge, was broadminded and full of zeal for modern organisation.[2] Apart from a palpitating moment for her staff when, all unwitting, I first called upon her unannounced in the *sancta sanctora* of the women's sections, we had few segregation difficulties and worked together with a will to introduce modern methods.

The first and most obvious thing to tackle was the method of paying the dividends on the very numerous small holdings of

2   Dame Myra Curtis DBE (1886-1971) joined the civil service in 1915. After the Post Office, she was appointed Assistant Secretary and Director of Women's Establishments at the Treasury, the most senior female position in the Civil Service at that time. She went on to prepare the Curtis Report in 1946, which resulted in the Children's Act 1948 requiring every local authority to set up a children's committee.

Government Stock held on what is termed 'the Post Office Register', as distinct from the larger Stock Exchange holdings administered by the Bank of England. This involved a clerical process twice a year that required copying particulars from voluminous lists onto separate dividend warrants, a double check to avoid clerical error and finally, enveloping and addressing by hand.

This was clearly a job for an addressing machine and cut-out envelopes: fortuitously, a new machine had just reached the market which would enable the warrants to be enveloped and sealed without further handling. But this was so profound a breach in the old order of things that had reigned for half a century that the Assistant Controller in charge protested violently that he felt unable to face the storm of indignation that he was sure would arise from stockholders when the new documents appeared. I tried to discover why he thought the public would object. The forms, it is true, would look a little different, but we could ensure that they would be readily accepted by the banks and at post offices. It seemed clear that only a genuine fear of change was at the root of his protest.

I asked the Assistant Controller when he usually took his holiday; he replied that he never did so until after the main batch of dividends had been despatched. So I offered him a fortnight of special leave while the new operation was carried through. A little to my surprise he accepted with alacrity. So, while the innovation was conducted, the officer in normal charge was in the south of France. The dividends went out and there was not a single objection. On his return he came to thank me for a good holiday and for relieving him of what he felt was an intolerable responsibility.

A more crucial operation was to enter the vast number of daily savings transactions in the centralised records of over a million individual accounts. They had been kept since the beginning in 1861 in large account books known as ledgers. These were buckram bound volumes some two feet in height and of varying thickness, which were ranged along massive desks and so contrived that they pivoted on their bottom edge onto the green baize slopes of the desks, narrowly missing the sunken inkpots used to make the entries by pen. Despite all the ingenuities of a Victorian half-century, this was no light task for the two thousand girls who spent their days thus employed. It was further aggravated by the need to check and recheck in a process of 'balancing' of all the manuscript entries, subject as they were to the inevitable element of error in a manual operation.

These were the days before computers had been developed, but mechanical accounting – or 'machine posting' – was well advanced. For the most part the problem came down to choosing between a galaxy of different manufacturers, all of them more than eager to demonstrate their wares and to capture one of the largest orders of its kind that had ever come their way.

The harder nut to crack was how to transfer the machine entries into those many elephantine ledgers which formed the meat and sinews of the bank. Clearly, these would need to be disembodied into some loose-leaf form; when this had been done, a host of problems would arise in the housing and handling of between a million and two million separate and distinct items – the largest card index in the world.

Steeped though it was in the traditions of the past, the Savings Bank staff took immense pride in the institution: it was a welcome and exhilarating experience to see how the teams of men and women, which we set up to investigate these problems, tackled their tasks and came up with the solutions.

One particular difficulty was to discover a card or paper capable of withstanding the immense amount of wear and tear over the years which operations of this nature would entail. The Stationery Office had nothing of the kind. Everything installed in quantity in other Government offices seemed to have become frayed or dog-eared in the course of time. Even the ubiquitous Savings Bank Deposit Book gave us no clue, despite experiments to move away from the sombre work-house image associated with it. It was the foreman of our printing works who provided the solution. Taking me aside when I was down in the works, he produced half a dozen well-used bank notes from his pocket and handed them to me. Rather puzzled, I asked him why?

'Well, sir.' he said. 'You said you were looking for a paper which wore well. What about these?' So I contacted Bernard Westall of De La Rue,[3] who had been one of my wartime Company Commanders. He said at once: 'Rag paper, that's what we and the Bank of England use for bank notes, and that ought to do the trick.' So rag it was (much of it pulped down from waste and from old foreign bank notes) that formed the basis of the new account cards in an unexpected fiscal resurrection.

Among many other changes which we made at this time, I set about improving and simplifying the forms used for corresponding with the public. I remember how they all ended with my signature after I became Controller, preceded by 'Your obedient Servant'. I remarked to my wife that I thought it looked old-fashioned.

'Well,' she said, 'I'd rather like to have a letter from you saying that you are my obedient servant, but if you like, "Yours faithfully" will do quite well'. So we adopted that subscription. It was later applied to all the Post Office correspondence forms; it also became the subject of the 'Yours faithfully, the Post Office' advertising campaign in an agitation arising from the introduction of First and Second Class Mail.

'Time makes ancient good uncouth'.[4] Many other changes made at this period have disappeared into the limbo of the past after the relocation of the Post Office Savings Bank to Glasgow and its transmogrification into a department of National Savings. However, the resulting economies were considerable – amounting in the case of the ledgers to a retrenchment of over 1,500 staff. The Treasury duly smiled benignly upon it all and allowed us to refurnish the vast football field of ledger rooms

3   Sir Bernard Clement Westall (1893-1970), served in the 10th Essex Regiment under DB during WW1. He joined De La Rue in 1922 as a junior clerk, and was appointed Assistant Managing Director in 1930, becoming Managing Director in 1934, and Chairman in 1944. He was responsible for turning De La Rue from an ailing British company into a successful international business. He was knighted in 1946. After DB retired from the Civil Service in 1946, Westall hired him as a Director of De La Rue, to further reinforce its international reputation.
4   Quote from 'The Present Crisis' by James Russell Lowell (1819-1891).

with a range of beautifully designed green roll-top steel cabinets: a show piece in the world of business efficiency and an immense pride to all concerned (including the Treasury). Pride of calling, pride in the institution, the firm or the regiment, is an immense motive force. The bank at Blythe Road, one large compact family, had always possessed this great pride of belonging. Now they succeeded in modernising themselves so completely and satisfactorily: their morale stood astonishingly high.

In the middle of 1932 there occurred one of those periodical international monetary crises that put this to a practical test. At the height of the First World War some £2,000 million of War Loan Stock was raised in a campaign of patriotic fervour. This huge sum then represented nearly a third of the national debt. With a coupon of 5%, naturally keyed interest rates – both at home and internationally – rose to an abnormally high rate.[5]

For some time Sir Montague Norman, the Governor of the Bank of England, had been semi-officially canvassing for the conversion of this debt to a lower rate. In early 1932 he persuaded the Treasury to attempt an audacious reduction by the conversion of the whole of the loan to 3½%.

Two factors were essential for success: complete secrecy and the speed of the operation.

Secrecy was a *sine qua non*. There was hardly a share in the market that would not be a certain bet for an immediate rise if it were guessed that the whole basis of gilt-edged was being altered. Even the Cabinet was not told in advance. It was said that the Chancellor subsequently apologised to them, saying that he did not think it feasible to pledge them to secrecy from their wives, nor reasonable to expect their wives to resist sharing such knowledge.

A few high officials in the Treasury and the Bank of England were informed, including the Controller of the Stationery

---

5 Due to the Depression, government revenues had declined to the extent that the interest repayments on this loan represented 40% of the income tax revenue (the term 'coupon' refers to the rate of interest paid by the Government on the loan).

Office. Beyond that, I was given to understand that I was one of the few other persons informed and that, on the Chancellor's instructions I was not to communicate it to my superiors at GPO, nor to the Postmaster General.

Speed in carrying out the operation was also considered a vital factor. Not only was the City conditioned technically and morally for a short, sharp shock, but the stockholders (the majority of them on the Post Office Register) were expected to respond more favourably to a rapid campaign.

Throughout the month of June 1932, it was like sitting on a barrel of gunpowder. The telephone was prohibited for any matter in this connection, and I was engaged in many subterfuges and deceits in visiting the Treasury to complete our preparations for this new July 1st Zero Hour.

On the evening of June 30th my plan was to warn a few selected staff to be prepared to stay behind for overtime – ostensibly to deal with the new machine posting. When the main body of the staff had left as usual in a remarkable human flood at 4:30 in the afternoon, the exit doors and gates of the building were locked and guarded. We then set about unwrapping and laying out the documents from the Stationery Office which had been secretly stored.

All the telephones were controlled and strict orders given that nobody might leave the building until the official announcement had been made in the House of Commons after the Stock Exchange had closed. Naturally, such drastic and unprecedented action produced its difficulties. One man, who had not left the office at his usual hour and had been imprisoned by the closing of the gates, steamed into my room and threatened to invoke the *Habeas Corpus Act* to secure his liberty. I explained matters to him and offered to telephone his wife or send the police round to explain that he had been detained at the office on some special work. But his wife was not the difficulty. It was another lady who was meeting him at a rendezvous. Happily, the hour arranged for the meeting was after the anticipated official announcement and I could promise him release in time, so *Habeas Corpus* was not needed. Nevertheless, it was with relief that I received a call a little later from Sir Warren Fisher from the Treasury to say the news was official, that all had gone satisfactorily, and that no whisper of it had leaked anywhere.

So we hurried to open the gates and release the captives, with a word of thanks to each as they streamed past into the evening. The cries of the newspaper sellers would confirm their alibis at home and assured them that they really had been front page news that evening.

Next day, July 1st, was another novel experience. The looks of amazement as the regular staff arrived at their places to carry out their normal tasks to find instead the whole office turned upside down and stacks of circulars and envelopes awaiting them at their usual workplaces, was a study in surprise. Indeed, it was a thrill to see them respond to the instruction and start folding and addressing as if their lives depended upon it. From the Controller to the newest messenger girl, everyone bent to the work; before long the trolleys were bulging with completed mail and trundling off to the Post Office Sorting Office. By four o'clock in the afternoon the job was done, the mail of over a million items posted and some bright spirits were indulging in an unprecedented, non-segregated and strictly unofficial dance in one of the tea-rooms.

What a *tour de force* for this great temple of routine! And what a tremendous shot-in-the-arm for the jaded financial times of the early thirties!

Alas! No redemption date was included in the terms of the 3½%, though there were voices even then who pleaded for it. And alas! the loan now stands at well under £50.[6]

---

6   Compared to the face value of £100, it would make no sense to pay it off – however due to the lack of redemption date, the government was obliged to keep paying 3.5% coupon (or interest) every year. It has been estimated that the government had paid £1.26bn in interest on these bonds since 1927. The Great War Loan bonds, worth nearly £2bn, were redeemed in full by Chancellor of the Exchequer, George Osborne, in 2014 to mark the centenary of WW1.

Lieutenant-Colonel Banks with the
13th London (Princess Louise's Kensington) Regiment

9

PRINCESS LOUISE'S

These were busy times, absorbing much energy – yet not all-absorbing, for it is a good maxim that advises, 'All work and no play, makes Jack a dull boy'. The more one's attention was confined to a particular activity, the more, I have found, it was desirable to seek an alternative occupation by way of relief and broadening an over-localised outlook.

This had been my original motive for joining the Yeomanry when I came first to London; the wheel now revolved full circle when I received a sounding from Sir Laming Worthington-Evans as to whether I could be available to take up the command of a suitable Territorial Army unit.

He told me later that, on arriving at the War Office as Secretary of State for War, he had been convinced by all the intelligence from abroad that the international cauldron was starting to simmer again and it behoved us to look to our defences. A new generation had arisen since the last hostilities and there was a general atmosphere of apathy and pacifism; recruiting was bad and, in particular the strength of the Territorial Army was much below a stable level. 'Worthy' always took the long view and, unlike Kitchener, was a believer in the Haldane model.[1] So, as a prime move, he was anxious to build up the gaps in the Territorial regiments.

He proposed various alternatives for me: there was a unit of my old Essex Regiment, but its headquarters were a long way away at Walthamstow; a Signals Regiment was also suggested, but did not seem very suitable as I had no technical experience. At this juncture, however, Lord Raglan completed his tenure of command of the 13th London (Princess Louise's Kensington)

---

1   Richard Haldane, Liberal Secretary of State for War (1905-12) was responsible for crucial reforms to the British Army before WW1. He created the Territorial Force (later Army) in 1908 as a means of enlisting volunteers to augment British land forces without conscription.

Regiment. The Colonel of the Irish Guards, commanding the Grey Brigade, sent for me and offered me the succession. It was almost ideal as the Headquarters were at Adam and Eve Mews, just off the Kensington High Street; furthermore, the Kensingtons were just the type of cockney soldier for which I had so much admiration and affection in my wartime unit.

So it was agreed, I was told to report to Adam and Eve (!) as soon as possible as Raglan was anxious to hand over.

Next evening, on my way home from work, I walked into this other Eden – a large, echoing and rather dingy drill hall – to be told by a rather perplexed Quartermaster that Lord Raglan had gone and what could he do for me?

It wasn't quite easy to answer, but as I sought haltingly to explain, a penny seemed to drop, the Quartermaster sprang to attention and said 'Won't you have a drink, Sir?' and led me to the Adjutant, Captain Gott, in the Officers' Mess.

'Strafer' Gott of the 60th Rifles was then doing his four years attachment as Adjutant and had some inkling of my appointment. So all was well and I joined the Kensingtons.

'Strafer', with his clear blue eyes (described by Sir Winston Churchill in *The Second World War*) had an air of diffidence that masked great ability and competence – as he was later to demonstrate in North Africa before his tragic end.[2] He was studying for entry to the Staff College, but in his modesty was doubtful about succeeding. It took all my persuasion to get him to persevere in his studies and to let me handle some of the multifarious detailed matters which normally fall to the lot of the permanent staff of a Territorial battalion in peacetime. His mere presence with the Kensingtons imparted a morale that foreshadowed the devotion which he earned from the Desert Rats in 1940. We never forgot the occasion when, late at night, the car in which he was being driven collided with a road island in the Kensington High Street. 'Strafer' got out, coolly put his

2   In 1942, General William Henry Ewart 'Strafer' Gott was appointed to lead the British 8th Army against Rommel in North Africa. On his way to Cairo to take up his command, his plane was repeatedly attacked by the enemy and he was killed.

thumb on the escaping fuel to prevent an explosion, and sent the driver off to fetch the police.

With Gott, some first-class NCOs from the Guards, a good cadre of officers and solid material in the ranks, there was every prospect of restoring the Kensington Regiment to its traditional high level. However, there was one snag: it was woefully under-strength.

In that respect it suffered from the blight of pacifism. Recruitment was mainly in the areas of Fulham (where the by-election result of 1933 frightened Baldwin into his pusillanimity on rearmament) and in Shepherd's Bush and Notting Hill where a man needed considerable courage to appear alone in uniform. Obviously, this required some so-called 'Public Relations'.

At that time this was something new to the Army. Except for the tornado of publicity which initiated Kitchener's Army, it had not been the Army practice to advertise for recruits. So we enlisted the Manager of the Shepherd's Bush Pavilion, Jimmy Forsyth, whose successful promotion methods at that cinema later took him to the top of the tree as Head of Gaumont-British Publicity.

'Have you got a band?' He asked immediately.

Well, there was quite a smart corps of drums, whose drum-major in civilian life was in charge of the lifts in Barker's Stores; he could throw a drum-major's staff as high as anyone, accompanied by the cries of the regiment: 'Going Up, Moddam!'

But Jimmy Forsyth wanted a full-blowing brass band as well, kitted out in the finery of the full-dress uniform of Grey and Scarlet. And this we had to find.

My friend the Quartermaster, Captain Cary, who was in charge of the sugar refinery of Tate and Lyle in Silvertown, thought he might be able to get the works band there to volunteer to join *en masse*. So for several Sundays I journeyed down to the docks to attend their practices and to talk it over with the men. They were generally favourable but, strongly corporate in spirit, stipulated that they should all join together and all be able to leave together if they so wished.

I consulted the Brigadier, Colonel Harold Alexander (later Earl Alexander of Tunis) who said sympathetically that he could know nothing officially of such a bargain, provided they joined as musicians; *ergo*, if the music went round and round and never came out,[3] they would cease to be efficient members of the regiment.

The other stipulation that they should all join together, however, proved more difficult. When, after several joint discussions it came to the vote, it proved impossible to get the piccolo player to agree to join. Several times we journeyed east on a Sunday to talk it over, but there was no budging him.

'It's his lady friend,' the others said. 'She thinks he's going off to the wars and she's going to lose him and his piccolo.' So I had to ask them if they would come without him ... and eventually they did.

There remained the problem of the full-dress uniforms, which – together with the drums – cost several thousand pounds. There was no hope of getting assistance from Army Funds, but Princess Louise gave us the leopard skins. As a further especially gracious gesture, she gave us her cipher badge, copied from a large silver replica on the cover of a blotter which, since the death of her husband, the Duke of Argyll, had reposed undisturbed on his desk in the study at their villa at Hardelot in France. The Honorary Colonel, Colonel Hugh Campbell, raised a sizeable contribution personally and from friends on the Stock Exchange. We collected the rest by appealing to prominent Kensingtonians and notably the inhabitants of Kensington Palace Gardens – 'Millionaire's Row' – which, incidentally, did not then include the Soviet Embassy.

So when the time came for the annual remembrance march to the Kensington War Memorial and the Cenotaph, we captured front page space in the picture papers, featuring our drums and band in the unusual full grey and scarlet uniform – handed down, it was said, from the *Fencibles* of the time of

---

3   A play on the lyrics of a popular song, written in 1935, and performed by artists such as Danny Kaye, Ella Fitzgerald and Tommy Dorsey: 'I blow through here/The music goes round and round/Whoo-ho-ho-ho-ho/And it comes out here...'

the Armada,[4] but certainly dating back for many years of the Volunteer movement.

As we swung out of Adam and Eve into the Kensington High Street to march past Princess Louise at the corner of Church Street, the regimental sergeant-major told me that the big drummer had not turned up from Silvertown, so not to turn the band on. It was a sad disappointment. But a few minutes later, as the column passed Derry and Toms, lo! Bandsman Bruce, in full regalia and bearing the big drum, emerged from South Kensington Station, where he had been held up on the Inner Circle Line, and manoeuvred himself skilfully into place in the band. With the traditional double-three boom of the drum, the band burst into the regimental march and the situation was saved.

We were now indeed a publicity-worthy spectacle and our unofficial Public Relations Officer, Jimmy Forsyth, decreed that we must be filmed for exhibition in the local cinemas and the *Gaumont News*. Our next annual training was held at Bordon in Hampshire. We arranged for the regiment to march from there to Hindhead. Thither the resourceful Jimmy preceded us with his cinema operator. After buying up a stock of small Union Jacks at the village Post Office (to which he had had a telegram sent to himself indicating the impending arrival of the Kensingtons on their 'Championship' march) he set forth to the local school, festooned with the flags. He then boldly asked the teacher if she would release the children for an hour to witness the arrival of the championship regiment. While she pondered this request, he started to distribute the flags to the children. And what child could resist either the flags or an unexpected holiday?

The day was won before the martial strains of the band were heard approaching: the schoolchildren, teachers, the postmistress and all the locals poured into the village High

---

4   A reference to the volunteer regiments raised in Britain and the colonies to defend against invasion during the Seven Years War, the American War of Independence, the Napoleonic Wars and the War of 1812. They were known as 'Fencibles' (from the word 'defencible'). It is questionable whether they operated under this name at the time of the Spanish Armada in 1588.

Her Royal Highness Princess Louise
with Lieut-Colonel Banks (right)
Kensington War Memorial, 4 November 1928

street while we plodded up the final hundreds of yards of that not inconsiderable hill of the Devil's Punch Bowl. We were greeted by a wild, flag-waving demonstration that surprised us as much as it did everyone else.

Jimmy got his film and didn't even charge us for the flags. 'Cheap at the price for Gaumont,' he said. 'Think what that footage would have cost in Hollywood.'

I never enquired about its distribution, nor its title; but I believe that it had an almost worldwide spread one week in the Gaumont and Pathé Gazettes.

So far as the Kensingtons were concerned, it featured as the star item at the Shepherd's Bush Pavilion one evening, when Princess Louise herself came to see it and was received by a Guard of Honour and an enthusiastic populace. An appeal for recruits was made from the stage: I have rarely been more nervous in my life, appearing in the limelight in uniform, medals and sword, and suspecting that our irrepressible PRO might have some further ploy in store. However, beyond a well-organised claque cheering my remarks to the echo while the National Anthem played in honour of Princess Louise, it all passed off well and we enlisted nearly 200 recruits as a result.

Sweet as this and other uses of publicity were, it was not quite enough: we still needed more to bring us up to strength and level-pegging with the ever-popular London Scottish in the Grey Brigade. So, led by my tireless Second-in-Command, Major (later Brigadier) Harold Prynne and with the aid of one of my keen Company Commanders (a partner in the well-known Estate Agency of J Trevor and Sons), we rounded up a number of temporarily empty shops in suitable parts of Fulham, Hammersmith and Notting Hill and showed 16mm editions of the famous film to any young men whom we could cajole into these extemporised recruiting booths. After a month of perhaps the most strenuous spare-time employment any of us had ever experienced, our ranks were full – and we had all learned a lot about public relations.

Sir Donald Banks, September 1935
(photo: Walter Stoneman,
courtesy National Portrait Gallery)

10

BACK TO ST MARTIN'S LE GRAND

I t seems to be a natural phenomenon that at regular, or irregular intervals in its history the General Post Office suffers a crisis of public criticism.

Represented directly in parliament by a Minister of the Crown, the GPO is closely geared to all the democratic processes of our parliamentary system. Yet strangely enough, it is remarkably unresponsive to public opinion, so that it appears to pontificate from its ivory tower in the City until as, for example, in the thirties of the 19th century and the thirties and sixties of the 20th century, a head of steam of unpopularity builds up and changes are forced upon it by extraneous means.

It would require an extensive study to analyse the reasons for this strange and in many ways inexplicable state of affairs. The usual, and by no means unreasonable, remedy proposed is to convert the institution into a commercial organisation and steps in that direction are now being contemplated paradoxically enough, by a Socialist administration.[1]

In 1932 there was one of these periodic crises of Parliamentary confidence, which crystallised in the publication of 'The Reform of the Post Office' by Viscount Wolmer, former Assistant PMG

---

1   Writing in the 1960s, DB is referring to the attempts in 1967 to transform the GPO into a public corporation under Harold Wilson's government. This culminated in the Post Office Act 1969, when the GPO became known as the Post Office, with separate divisions for post and telecommuncations. The position of Postmaster General was abolished, but the main board appointments continued to be made by the government, and the opportunity to separate the postal and telecommunications activities into autonomous organisations was compromised. This separation was achieved in 1984, when British Telecom was floated on the London Stock Exchange. The transition to public company was eventually completed in 2011 with the flotation of the Royal Mail.

to Sir William Mitchell-Thompson in 1924. His criticisms were in the main directed at the vertical structure which divided the modern and more technical telephones and telegraphs from the older postal services. To this were added suggestions of greater flexibility through decentralisation and complete financial independence for the Post Office. He also recommended that its identification with the revenue-raising departments should be supplanted by the principle of making it pay its own way.

Sir Kingsley Wood, who had been Parliamentary Private Secretary to Neville Chamberlain at the Ministry of Health, was appointed Postmaster General in 1933. He at once set up a strong committee under Lord Bridgeman, with Lord Cadman of the Anglo-Persian Oil Company, to review the whole question. They held their enquiries in the august and characteristically Victorian room on the first floor of GPO North known as the 'Deputation Room'. It was a daunting experience to be summoned before them in that room, its walls covered with portraits of nearly a hundred former Postmasters General.

For years since my return from France I had taken a keen interest in the study of organisations. John Lee, Controller of the Central Telegraph Office, was a well-known authority on public service organisation.[2] We used to spend our holidays together: as well as discussing these matters, we also spent a good deal of time digging into the many variations which were beginning to form subject matter for the Institute of Public Administration. Lyn Urwick too, a noted expert on organisations, was a friend of mine and had contributed much to these ideas and their practical application to the GPO.[3] So I found little difficulty

2   John Lee CBE MA MComm (1867-1928) was the first Editor of the *Journal of Public Administration*. He published a number of books on telegraphs and management theory, including *The Principles of Industrial Welfare* (1924) and lectured at Oxford and Cambridge on these subjects.
3   Lyndall Fownes Urwick (1891-1983) was a management consultant in the emerging field of business administration. He was influential in the acceptance that management, as with other disciplines, was made up of a set of skills that could be taught. He went on to work with Banks at the Petroleum Warfare Department in WW2, during which time he published *Elements of Business Administration* (1943). In their spare time, they

in propounding solutions to the committee and found them very interested and receptive. When, after repeated sessions, I escaped back to Blythe Road, I concluded in review that either I had exceeded all the bounds of loquacity, or that something in truth was about to come of it. Which indeed it was!

The Bridgeman Committee reported in favour of a scheme of regionalisation, tying together the varied functions under Regional Directors responsible for all the Post Office Services in their regions and not solely those of the Posts, as had been the case under Anthony Trollope's 'Surveyor' system of the past. It recommended the independence of Post Office finances, subject to an annual fixed sum contribution to the Exchequer of £10,000,000 to cover taxation and other servicing charges: the balance earned over this period being allocated at the Department's discretion to the improvement of its services. Conspicuously, it also proposed abolishing the old post of 'Secretary to the Post Office': instead, that the Permanent Head should become a Chief Executive with the title of Director General.

To those in the department, this was the most intriguing proposal of all. Sir Evelyn Murray, who had held the Secretaryship for nearly twenty years, was nothing if not a traditionalist and it was unlikely that he would continue in the new circumstances. Who would succeed him?

In the past it had usually been a Treasury appointment, but some hints that had been let fall by the Committee supporting the possibility of an inside selection. The speculation was intense.

I had been having a series of personal discussions on Savings Bank advertising with Sir Kingsley Wood when, suddenly, one morning out of the blue, I received a summons to lunch with him at his home at Tunbridge Wells. This was unusual procedure, but I stuffed my despatch case with appropriate papers and proceeded to Victoria. At Tunbridge Wells the Postmaster General met me in his own car and increased my curiosity by asking me a number of questions about my career

conceived and established the foundations for the Administrative Staff College (later Henley Business School).

and the careers of a number of my colleagues. Then, when we arrived, he took me into the large billiard room, full of original Low cartoons of himself and his contemporaries, told me to put my despatch case aside and asked me if, as a soldier, I had learnt to obey orders. I said I had. 'Well,' he said, 'this is an order from the Prime Minister, from the Permanent Head of the Civil Service and from myself. You are to take over from Sir Evelyn Murray as Director General of the Post Office, and I want you to do so on Monday of next week.'

On the journey back to Victoria I was preoccupied with very different thoughts and speculations from those of my outward journey. This was indeed a fantastic climax to my first limping arrival at the GPO – a span of fifteen years from the lowest rung to the top of the ladder, at an age in the early forties. It was an immense task but one abounding in possibilities. There were colleagues who would be sadly disappointed in being superseded by someone much junior to them in service. Above all, there was the unhappy prospect of the personal displacement of my old chief, Sir Evelyn Murray, in the post which he had held so long and, in the eyes of those who served with him, so uniquely.

So it was with much perturbation that I presented myself the next Monday at the familiar Private Secretary's door at St Martin's le Grand, surveyed the great man through the peephole and was ushered into the presence by Lumley (later Sir Dudley Lumley KBE). Murray looked up pensively, swept his hand over a small pile of papers on one corner of his desk and said:

'That's all there is for you at the moment. I dare say there will be a lot more before long, but Lumley will put you in the picture. Well, the best of luck, Banks. I've always wished you well, and you need those wishes more than ever now.'

And he gathered up his top hat and *The Times* and walked out to the Customs and Excise.[4] The place seemed to go chilly and unreal, and I looked quickly round for the magic PS button

4   Sir Evelyn Murray (1880-1947) became Chairman of the Board of Customs and Excise in 1934, a position which he held until his retirement in 1940.

to press and summon Lumley from the outer regions – indeed, almost as if I were hoping for some consolation.

My predecessor had only just left the building when I was summoned by Sir Kingsley Wood down to the PMG's room on the floor below. Here he welcomed me, benignly seated at the head of a long massive table, usefully employed for conferences when required, but in fact designed in the spacious days when the old Duke of Norfolk was Postmaster General for the purpose of laying out the minutes successively for his signature, so that he could sign them while he partook of a glass of port which awaited his noon arrival. After completing his documentary perambulation with the minimum expenditure of time and effort, he was able to depart from his duties in ample time for lunch.[5]

This, however, was a very different time and tempo and Kingsley Wood was anxious to let no interval elapse before making a clear and evident change of approach. As at a later date, when he succeeded Lord Swinton at the Air Ministry, he was insistent on the need to use the immediate impact of public relations.

In Sir Laming Worthington-Evans' time, the GPO had been the first government department to appoint a regular public relations officer. I remember some shaking of heads at this new phenomenon and predictions that in the future we should see it magnified across the whole spectrum of government and attempts made to supplant normal political methods by such mechanisms.

This first essay at the Post Office tended early to confirm such forecasts as Chapman, the new PRO, soon fell victim to that insatiable appetite for the limelight which is inseparable from the world of politics. Chapman had a knowledge of Fleet Street but

---

5   In his memoirs, Tony Benn recalls how DB told him this anecdote at a gathering of retired Postmasters General and Directors General in the 1960s. However, Benn incorrectly attributed the ceremony to Kingsley Wood rather than the Duke of Norfolk. This error was compounded when Duncan Campbell-Smith repeated the Benn version in *Masters of the Post: the authorised history of the Royal Mail*.

not so much of Westminster. When he issued a harmless official handout in the PMG's name, he fell into the trap of appending, for the benefit of reporters, a favourable biographical note of Worthington-Evans' political history. This was pounced upon by the party critics and, knowing that Worthy had aspirations for higher office in the cabinet, it was assumed that he was using the new official machinery for his personal ends. All this caused much furore in the press and a nine-days sensation in what became headlined as 'the Worthy Puff'. Poor Chapman disappeared in the brouhaha but left the lesson behind him. And Kingsley Wood was careful to appoint an experienced and outstandingly wise PRO, Jack Brebner, who piloted us through the many reefs and shoals, and later did outstanding service during the war at the Ministry of Information.

Kingsley Wood, Jack Brebner and Sir Stephen Tallents, who came to us from the Colonial Office, made a remarkable team. Kingsley had the most outstanding gift of awareness of what the public thought and wanted. Though virtually an abstainer, he used to go into public houses to sense the current of public opinion; he also kept a kit of an old suit and a cloth cap so as to mingle unnoticed with the crowds on occasions of public demonstrations. It was interesting to compare him with Lord Beaverbrook: two supreme publicists – one firmly entrenched in the minds of the people, the other personally confident in knowing people's minds; but, with his newspaper behind him, Beaverbrook seemed more concerned with what he wanted them to think and in making up their minds for them.

Stephen Tallents brought with him the simple and unobtrusive outlook of the typical Englishman. Later, at John Reith's instance, he was appointed to the BBC and was intrstrumental in promoting Richard Dimbleby and all that Dimbleby stood for in the fostering of great traditions there.[6]

Kingsley Wood took the line that what was of primary importance to change the public image of the Post Office through a campaign directed at restoring the pride and confidence of

6　Richard Dimbleby was the BBC's first war correspondent and, with the advent of TV, a leading news commentator. He died in 1965.

the staff themselves, whose morale had been shaken by years of complaint and criticism.

It happened that the engineers had just perfected a device, now known as the Speaking Clock, which enabled a telephone subscriber to ascertain the time by dialling TIM. But a voice was needed and this is where Kingsley Wood came in. 'You must find the most charming telephonist's voice we have,' he insisted. 'Not only will it set the standard by which the whole of the service will measure itself but, given the right kind of charm, perhaps collect a few extra calls from lonely bachelor subscribers yearning romantically for that excellent thing in woman, a voice ever soft, gentle and low.'

So the 'Girl with the Golden Voice' competition was born. Exchange competed with exchange throughout the country. By enlisting subscribers as judges, the competing girls were gradually eliminated. We tried at the same time to develop a competition for the 'Perfect Subscriber' but the interest of the press and public was concentrated on the girls and, as some cynic remarked, perhaps the perfect subscriber is simply 'Patience on a monument'.

The dozen or so finalists for the Golden Voice event were brought to London where a small panel of well-known actors and actresses judged their elocution: the girls were concealed behind a screen, and a large number of pressmen and photographers waited in the auditorium for the result. It was a tense and exciting performance and happily one girl in particular seemed to have all the gold of the skies in her voice. As the judges were coming to their decision, Brebner looked more and more anxious and whispered to Kingsley, 'I hope she's not an ugly one!' 'Ask Dame Sybil Thorndike (who was one of the judges)' he said. Dame Sybil nodded comprehendingly, stole behind the screen and emerged a few seconds later with her thumbs up. It was all right. They had chosen, not only the best voice but the best looker. And so TIM and the Speaking Clock got its golden voice and the winning telephonist emerged to be overwhelmed by a wave of reporters and photographers – a precursor to the Miss World beauty contests which started in 1951.

I remember becoming a little concerned afterwards about the effect all this ballyhoo might have upon an unsophisticated exchange girl; so I got Lumley to arrange for her to see me before she went back to the provinces. Explaining that she might get a number of film or other offers, I advised her to have them carefully vetted by a lawyer before she signed anything. She thanked me, looked at me rather hard, bobbed a quaint little curtsey, and disappeared hurriedly. I asked Lumley what happened. 'Oh!' he said 'She thought you wanted to make a pass at her yourself. I don't think that you need worry: she wasn't born yesterday.'

The size and ubiquity of the General Post Office, with a staff of a quarter of a million and establishments in every part of the country, were formidable factors. I set myself the task of trying to visit them all in my time as Director General. But as there were 23,000 Post Offices and I was some 43 years of age, it worked out that I should need to visit something like a thousand a year if I were to complete the task before retirement. Nevertheless, I started on the programme and got a respectable distance in the first few years.

I took the PMG with me when it could be conveniently arranged. A visit to the City exchanges with Kingsley Wood in the latter part of a business morning was particularly fruitful. As the lunch-hour approached the flashing lights on the boards died down and one could almost see the City reaching for its hat and going out to lunch. 'What time do they come back?' Kingsley asked. 'Well, we don't get really busy again until between three and five,' the Supervisor told us, 'Then they all seem to call at once and go home and the boards go practically dead until next morning.'

Kingsley looked thoughtful and asked me afterwards to find out how the traffic graph went for the whole country. It was obvious that the equipment had to be adequate to cope with the top peak loads; but in between these, and particularly after normal working hours, it was standing idle and not earning its keep. Could we not utilise this and attract additional custom by offering special off-peak rates?

This was the genesis of the Shilling Call anywhere in the country. The accountants set to work to study the resultant costs of additional long-distance off-peak traffic and came up with the answer of between ten and eleven pence. 'A Shilling is the right charge!' said the Postmaster General. Somewhat in the manner of a Telephone Rowland Hill, he set about introducing the Shilling Call anywhere in the British Isles as the universal maximum after 6pm.

There were exciting times when the new charges began. Between Aberdeen and London the former rates had been seven and six pence and it was not long before the traffic for trunk calls by the Aberdeen business man shifted to a pattern of remarkable evening pressure. Just what those Aberdonians did in the daytime, I don't know. But they caused us the greatest anxiety to prevent the relatively few connecting long-distance lines to London being swamped with telephonic euphoria as 6 pm struck. For several nights I went across to the trunk exchange at Faraday House to watch the flickering lights growing in intensity at the Aberdeen position; gradually the engineers managed to set up relief circuits and even route some of the calls through Northern Ireland, until the first enthusiasms in Aberdeen diminished and this critical situation was mastered.

Elsewhere, of course, there were momentary difficulties but the reduced rates were so generally welcomed that the public sympathy was with us and Brebner was able to give Fleet Street a good story. Our most severe critics, I found afterwards when I visited the United States, were the telephone authorities there who considered that we had not quite played the game, since there was no chance that they would be able to introduce such low universal rates on the North American continent. One leading member of the AT&T administration would hardly speak to me about it when I arrived, as they were then suffering under a Congressional enquiry into their own rates. I had great difficulty in persuading him even to consider investigating with us the development of an Atlantic telephone cable, which later took the place of the less satisfactory radio link. I think he feared we might seek to bring in a shilling telephone call to America!

His adverse reaction, however, was professional rather than personal: with much generosity AT&T allowed me free telephoning anywhere in the Bell system while I was in the USA. This gesture did much to thaw out the initial coolness and before I left New York we had together worked out some substantial reductions in international telephone rates, which the GPO was able to parallel in all its overseas services in due course.

Our talks involved some interesting discussions on telephone charges in general in which, as might be expected, the American view tended towards the doctrine of 'what the traffic will bear'. Against that it could be argued that the lower the charges the greater the traffic and correspondingly (within limits) the greater the revenue. This in general was the guiding policy in the Kingsley Wood days and it usually yielded satisfactory results, although there was necessarily much that was empirical about it. Learned papers are still being written by experts and university professors, but the last word on this – in Britain at least – has not yet been said. Unlike the Americans and the Canadians, we are not conditioned in these islands to the universality of the telephone, although in recent years it has come to be accepted that a telephone to every household is a desirable policy aim.[7]

To that end, Kingsley Wood experimented with cheaper rentals and installation charges. The expedient of a limited number of free calls was also introduced with the object of reducing the liability of a low-income subscriber for his rental, while still affording him the use of the system for emergency purposes and incoming calls. This, however, never worked out quite satisfactorily. Human nature, and particularly female human nature, finds the temptation to use the telephone, once installed, irresistible: the number of free calls was almost inevitably exceeded.

One of the most forward-thinking of later PMGs, Mr Wedgwood Benn, was exceedingly keen to try to extend the

---

7   In 1970, 35% of UK households had a landline, rising to 95% by the end of the 20th century. This figure has declined ever since due to the number of mobile phones (https://www.statista.com/statistics/289158/telephone-presence-in-households-in-the-uk/).

availability of the phone to elderly householders living on their own but, short of subsidising these lines, he found it impracticable to find the solution before he was moved to the higher spheres of technology.

Under Kingsley Wood another improvement was a substantial increase of public call boxes. Like almost every new PMG, he was dissatisfied with the existing style of telephone kiosks and sought a new design. At that time the kiosks, made of grey concrete, were – in our view – most unattractive; but when I raised the question with the responsible officials at the GPO, they assured me that only a comparatively short time before one of the leading architects of the day had been commissioned to produce the design we disliked so much. This was a bit of a problem: it was only after much consideration that I decided to take the bull by the horns and appeal to the architect himself.

When he called on me I explained, rather diffidently, how we felt about the current design; while I was doing so his face lit up and he interjected: 'My dear Sir. Please say no more. Every time I pass one of these creations of mine I feel worse and worse about it. You would be doing me the greatest kindness if you would allow me to submit a new design which I should be happy to do without any charge at all.' So all was well: the present tall red kiosk – now almost as familiar as the red pillar box – was substituted. Although not always acclaimed, it has in general assimilated itself to our national landscape. Some public controversy arose about the colour and a few variations of green or stone-grey were permitted in particular beauty spots, such as Corfe Castle and the Cotswolds. Kingsley Wood's own contribution – a mirror inside for the ladies – was, I hardly need say, psychologically impeccable.[8]

8   The K6 or Jubilee kiosk was designed by Sir Giles Gilbert Scott in 1935. Less expensive to produce and more aesthetically pleasing than its predecessor, the Post Office rolled the kiosks out nationwide to celebrate the King George V Jubilee. Between 1935 and 1968 some 60,000 K6 kiosks were installed across the UK. There was a public outcry when British Telecom started to phase out the underused kiosks in the 1980s, and as a result many were retained by local communities. 11,700 remain in use of which 2,500 are Grade-2 listed. In 2006, in a poll on Britain's most iconic designs by the

There were many other telephone matters, such as the adoption and ordering up of the automatic systems which have become almost universal, and the introduction of the 999 emergency call. As well, the extension of installation facilities to the remotest parts of the country – paralleling the postal developments of 1897 – which in themselves were enough to keep me at full stretch.

My *alter ego*, Sir Thomas Gardiner, with a wealth of postal experience as Controller of the London Postal Service, came in as Deputy Director General to handle the very considerable task of reorganisation and reconstruction envisaged by the Bridgeman Committee. In the old order of things the local Postmaster and the local telephone and engineering officials worked independently, indeed hardly knew each other. Matters affecting both sides would require to be referred all up the ladder to London for settlement at a higher level. This was anathema to the public and caused much criticism; so it was arranged to appoint regional directors, chosen impartially from either side, with authority to deal with and settle local affairs rapidly within the region. After extensive trials and exhaustive discussion with the staff and officials concerned, Gardiner evolved a flexible and effective structure based on the old Surveyor system. This was to withstand all the strains and stresses of the testing times of the 1939-1945 war and, it might be claimed, virtually removed the pre-war bugaboos besetting the Post Office organisation. It was a *tour de force* in decentralisation. Alas! It now seems that with the impending break-up of the GPO into separate and distinctive Corporations and Ministries, a fresh *tour de force* will be necessary to avert the very evils which Bridgeman and Gardiner strove to eliminate.

Apart from this structural reform little innovation was introduced on the postal side at this time. The Posts were in a flourishing condition financially and, generally speaking, less in need of attention than Telecommunications. Some measures were instituted to ensure that late afternoon posting in London

Design Museum and BBC Television, the K6 kiosk was voted into the top ten by the British public.

and the big cities secured first delivery anywhere except in the remoter country districts, by next morning; some tentative steps were also taken to experiment with mechanical sorting of letters – all of which suffered setbacks when war broke out in 1939.

The most obstinate problem of all was the Telegraph Service. This had always been a money-loser: Kingsley Wood pulled out all the stops in the organ, but the magic would not work. We tried reducing rates by offering a sixpenny telegram: the traffic responded favourably, yet the increase was insufficient to compensate for the loss of revenue.

A close analysis of telegrams showed a comparatively limited and inelastic range of uses. Their main use was for social or congratulatory purposes and it was this side which appeared capable of development.

Eventually, we decided to see what could be done by introducing a Good News, or Greetings service. Unfortunately for the telegraphs, the image of the telegram had become blackened by its association with death. During the Great War relatives of those who were killed were notified by wires sent from the War Office. For years after the return of peace, my mother used to shudder at the sight of a messenger boy bearing an ominous brown envelope. So the first thing was to destroy that unhappy association of ideas by enveloping good news in such a way that it heralded itself happily. A striking gold envelope (later supplemented by silver envelopes for weddings) was adopted for the greetings message. I had the pleasure of sending one of the first of these to my mother on her birthday with the happiest of effects. Indeed, the Greetings Telegram, introduced by Kingsley Wood's successor Lord Tryon to show that he was continuing the traditions of his predecessor, was one of the most effective features of his regime and fostered something of a new social habit. It is commemorated in the unusual heraldic supporter of a telegraph messenger in the coat of arms which embellishes his memorial in the little country church of Durnford in Wiltshire.

To Lord Tryon also fell the task of handling the new postage stamp issued on the accession of King Edward VIII. There is an apocryphal story that, before he appoints a Postmaster

General, the Prime Minister first satisfies himself that he is not a philatelist. But every PMG who comes to the office is inevitably interested in the design of stamps. In Sir Kingsley Wood's time there was no special occasion requiring a change in the current somewhat complicated design of the King George V issue; but, seizing the opportunity afforded by the Silver Jubilee in 1935, he put forward to the Palace the proposal for a commemorative stamp, designed by Barnett Freedman. This was approved by King George V – a keen stamp collector – after he had rejected, in salty language, some specimens of photographic reproductions of his head in favour of the traditional sculptured form.

It was no doubt something more than a coincidence that, not long after my appointment as Director General, I was commanded to attend an afternoon party at Buckingham Palace. Shortly after my arrival, I was singled out by the King and taken to a settee away from the other guests where he told me of his stamp collection.

'I only collect British and Commonwealth stamps,' he said. 'And the other day a man died who had claimed that he had the best collection in the world. So I sent Bacon (Sir Edward Bacon, his Curator of Stamps) to see it and he came back and said it wasn't a patch on mine!'

His enthusiasm was engaging but I felt quite embarrassed to be monopolising his attention, until Queen Mary came over and, looking understandingly at me, said 'George, George, I suppose you are talking about your old stamps. Now, come along and entertain your other guests. And don't you give him any stamps, Sir Donald.'

Sadly enough, there were few opportunities for giving him any for he only survived the Silver Jubilee by a little over a year. With the memory of his interest and as a means of raising funds for his memorial, an exceptional tribute was prepared in the form of a purple mourning stamp, printed with a prominent inscription IN MEMORY in a 1½d denomination, which it was proposed to put on sale at Post Offices for a limited time.

It was a striking stamp, but the new Sovereign showed little interest in the proposal and it was dropped. Instead, we were urged to make all haste to get the new Edward VIII issue out in time for it to be in use before the Coronation. This was a tough proposition as, on previous occasions, the new issue of coinage and postage stamps had been synchronised with the Coronation. Furthermore, there was at that time an impenetrable screen over the intended date for King Edward's Coronation. However, we set about preparing a photographic model, rather larger than standard size: with some simplification in the wording and framework, it gave promise of a very striking design. With specimens of this in his pocket and attired in tail-coat and topper, Lord Tryon set forth to the palace to secure King Edward's approval. Unfortunately he also slipped some other different alternatives in his pocket and, on the King's insistence, produced these for His Majesty who seized upon them and said he wanted to show them to someone before he finally decided. When they came back we found to our dismay that that someone had selected the version which we had discarded, with the King's profile looking from light to darkness and no crown over his head. Nothing that the PMG could do was able to alter Mrs Simpson's choice, so the fateful stamp went into circulation with all its unhappy auguries.

Each political period tends to develop its particular *leitmotifs*: just as technology and computing have been the theme in recent years, the prevailing emphasis between the wars was on the air and its importance – both in its application to commercial and to military purposes.

Imperial Airways – after a comparatively modest start with a service between London and Paris – was now seeking fresh scope for air development under the dynamic leadership of Sir Eric Geddes and his able managing director George Woods-Humphreys. Backed by the active imagination of Sir Christopher Bullock at the Air Ministry, they turned to the Post Office as a means of providing freight and revenue for worldwide expansion.

There were two principal objectives: the most striking was what was termed the 'All-up Empire Air Mail', which had considerable strategic implications both in communications and in providing finance for large-scale transport aircraft.

Parallel with this was the goal of a Transatlantic Air Service which, as things turned out, was of more urgent significance in my early days with Kingsley Wood at the GPO.

Pan American Airways and the United States authorities tended strongly to favour an Atlantic route which would bring the service into Europe direct and avoid Great Britain; but the span of the ocean involved was at that time barely within the capacity of available aircraft engines, particularly in the face of prevailing winds. The Azores were a possibility as a staging-point but suffered from poor landing facilities.

The British Government favoured a northerly line which would mean that the main traffic routes would follow the Great Circle across the narrows of the North Atlantic into Britain. This proposal was strongly supported by the Irish Free State[9] – eager to develop their projected airport at Shannon – as well as Newfoundland and to a lesser extent by Canada.

From the postal point of view there was not much in it, one way or the other, although the Canadian link to complete the empire scheme was naturally attractive. More cogent, however, were the pressures that Pan-American were applying both in the White House and in air circles, to get a settlement in favour of the Azores, Lisbon and Paris. Our Commonwealth authorities became alarmed; as a result I was hastily put in charge of a mission representing Whitehall and the Air Ministry. Two able representatives from the Irish Free State joined us at Liverpool, whence we sailed for Montreal in a Canadian Pacific ship and set ourselves to study all the facets of the new aerial bridge. Finance necessarily loomed large: transport of mail by sea had occupied a prominent place in postal history since the institution of the sea packets under the Admiralty in the 19th Century; it was comparatively inexpensive. Transport by air required that greater consideration be given to weight; coupled with the greater intrinsic costs of aerial transport, this raised new fiscal questions. The contest was mainly between

9   The Irish Free State was established in 1922 when 26 of the 32 counties of Ireland formed an independent state following the Anglo-Irish Treaty of 1921. The Free State existed until 1937, when it became known as Ireland.

the conventional postal school of thought, which held that it was the primary duty of postal services to deliver mail by the quickest means without exacting extra charges for speed, and the air operators who were anxious to obtain the extra revenue accrued through a surcharge. The battle raged until we sighted the icy shores of Labrador and entered the St Lawrence Estuary, where the ingenious Woods-Humphreys, extemporising the first model of an 'Aerogramme', or Air Letter Form from a piece of CPR notepaper, threw that suggestion into the discussion and turned the scales in favour of a surcharge for conveying air mail across the Atlantic. Thus it happened that for most overseas air mails there were postage rates, although within the British Isles and Europe letters were sent by air at surface rates of postage if earlier delivery was thereby achieved.

The salient factor in the controversy concerning routes was the firm determination of the Irish representatives, and of a very dogged John Leydon in particular, to put Ireland and the great Shannon Airport they planned on the Transatlantic Air map. I never think of that great enterprise amid the wastes of the Limerick countryside without the memory of that tenacious and altogether lovable little Irishman and his devotion to his great ideal. The leprechauns somehow came into his case, and he would argue, 'After all, we had to leave Ireland for the New World in the days of trouble. And now it's only right and proper that Ireland herself should be able to be the first to welcome her own when they fly home after all these years.'

Time and technical progress in air transportation have, of course, put different values on the geographical situation of Shannon Airport. However, our arrival in North America at that point, closely linked for the first time with the Irish Free State, was a strong card in favour of the mission. The American newspapers commented on the unusual sight of the Union Jack and the flag of the Irish Free State flying side by side outside the Mayflower Hotel where we stayed in Washington.

It was this strongly welded alliance in the mission that enabled us to face a somewhat curious lack of sympathy on the part of the Canadian authorities to the conception of the

Northern Route. To our way of thinking, it was only to be expected that Canada would welcome inclusion in the joint facilities, with Montreal and Toronto as gateways into the large centres of American population around the Great Lakes. But Prime Minister Mackenzie King had an historical reluctance to accept what he seemed to regard as an attempt by Britain to intervene in Canadian affairs. With C D Howe, the friendly and encouraging Canadian Minister of Transport, I was able to do something to help in the initial steps of setting up TransCanada Air Lines as the instrument by which Canada would participate in the Atlantic services. But even his advocacy did not clear up all the difficulties.

Mackenzie King at that time was away from Ottawa taking medical treatment in Georgia, and he had some resentful representations conveyed direct to London on what he considered to be undue pressure by the mission to participate in our conclusions A very expensive telephone call from London, lasting three-quarters of an hour, resulted when Sir Harry Batterbee of the Colonial Office called me up at the Chateau Laurier Hotel in Ottawa to discuss these representations. I consulted John Leydon who said he was quite prepared to go on to Washington without Canadian participation if they so desired, provided that it was clear that Canada was no longer included in the reciprocal arrangements. So we went to the next meeting at the Canadian headquarters and he exploded the bombshell. It took almost an all-night session during which, I fancy, the wires to Warm Springs became very busy. But in the end Canada signed and we proceeded as a united mission, together with Canada, to secure the agreement of the Washington authorities in establishing a twice weekly round trip service between North America and Britain via Shannon, with rights of participation by all the signatory countries.

It was still touch and go, for F D Roosevelt himself was still hankering after the southerly route. As leader of the mission I had to pay a courtesy call on the President in his famous little Oval Office in the White House. Sitting there under the Presidential banners, he congratulated the mission on its successful results, although, fairly clearly, he did not seem to be fully informed in detail. Then, in a mood of reminiscence, he said: 'You know, when I was Secretary to the Navy in the war, I was once offered the Presidency of the Azores.' Sensing we were on delicate ground, I took a chance and asked him if he regretted that he had not taken that one instead of the one he now held. He burst into a peal of laughter. 'Well,' he said, 'I reckon it would have been a bit easier.' To my relief we skated off the subject of the Azores.[10]

10 The President's diary records that the ten-minute meeting took place at 11:40am on 11 December 1935 (http://www.fdrlibrary.marist.edu/daybyday/daylog/december-11th-1935/).

Sir Donald Banks, 9 March 1938
(photo: Bassano Ltd,
courtesy National Portrait Gallery)

11

AIR MINISTRY

After those adventures across the Atlantic, I suppose it was only natural that, when Sir Christopher Bullock left the Air Ministry in 1936, I was selected to replace him as Permanent Under-Secretary.

It was not an appointment that I welcomed, as there was still a great deal to be done at the GPO. Indeed, it seemed as if I was only just getting into my stride there. On the other hand, Gardiner was fully able to take over the remainder of the work we had started together and, with the vast expansion of the German air force looming menacingly in the political field, the Air Ministry was a very key appointment.

Apart from the relative importance of both jobs, there is a great difference in practice between civil service permanent heads in defence departments and those in other government departments. In the latter – to quote Winston Churchill – distinction which he offered in a famous debating quip to translate for the benefit of any Old Etonians present, they are *facile princeps*; but in the Navy, Army or Air Force Boards they are not even *primus inter pares*. In these boards the civil chief – apart from his role as political adviser to the minister – is little more than a financial watchdog.

I have no close knowledge of how the Army Council or the Board of Admiralty works in that respect, but on the Air Council at this period, the function of the Secretary to the Air Ministry was almost wholly secretarial. Military air policy, apart from requirements, naturally was the primary and essential concern of the Chief of the Air Staff and the Air Council, and I can recollect no occasion when broad air force policy as such was specifically discussed in council. One military question which did arise was the retention of rifles by the RAF. I recall being asked by an air marshal – perhaps because I was the only infantryman present – whether I thought that the rifle was any longer of use!

The great and all-important question however behind all the political agitation at that time, and all the schemes for expansion, was the degree to which priority should be given to fighter aircraft compared with bombers. This matter was rarely if ever touched upon in meetings of the Air Council. The decisions in favour of a preponderance of bombing machines were hammered in separate service discussions – influenced to a remarkable degree by the continual pressure exercised by Lord Trenchard behind the scenes.

Trenchard has been deservedly called 'The Father of the Royal Air Force.' Never, at any time, did he cease to watch over it with a paternal eye. If the RAF failed to have a representative alongside their corresponding members of the navy or the army at an important function in the City, the Air Member for Personnel would have his elbow jogged from Brooks' Club: here Boom[1] held a secondary court charged with keeping the air force and the strategical aims of the bomber offensive impressed on all and sundry. In this he had the clerical assistance of a civilian member of the Air Ministry. Sometime after I had been appointed Permanent Civil Head of the Ministry, I learnt with a sense of shock that this officer was strictly forbidden to impart any of this information to me.

The atmosphere in the ministry was correspondingly difficult. Under Lord Swinton's outstanding drive and leadership there was tremendous enthusiasm and devotion in building up the 'shadow' aircraft factories all over the country. A privileged few of us used to make our regular pilgrimages to a secret chart room where I arranged a vivid graphical display, plane by plane, of the feverish rearmament of the RAF: the old biplanes being represented in red with the newly produced monoplane models in blue replacing them as the machines arrived at the squadrons. I think it was some time after Munich that the changeover was completed and the chart room had turned completely from red to blue. At the time of Munich the comparative paucity of modern fighters was one of the factors which influenced

---

1   Lord Trenchard's nickname.

Mr Chamberlain's policy of appeasement, and it was most disquieting to some of us in the Ministry to find little change in the attitude of the 'Bomber School'.

As Lord Ismay remarks in his *Memoirs*[2]

> As war loomed nearer and nearer, it was proposed from time to time that the number of fighter squadrons should be increased. But the Air Ministry were opposed to this unless the number of bomber squadrons was simultaneously increased in proportion.
>
> They said the multiplication of fighters was a heresy which appealed only to those who were ignorant about air power and did not understand that the counter-offensive by bombers must always be our crowning aim.
>
> In theory they may have been perfectly correct, but to the layman it seemed ... that the vital need was to ensure that the Citadel could be effectively defended until we could build up the necessary apparatus – including of course large numbers of bombers – to assume the offensive.

Lord Swinton was well aware of the importance of defensive measures and set up the Tizard Committee to explore the scientific possibilities for Air Defence. Thanks to their encouragement of Watson-Watt's[3] early essays with radar at Teddington, I was charged by Swinton to make a special appeal to the Treasury for the necessary funds for radar defences on a comprehensive scale across the whole east coast. It was a welcome relief in an otherwise baffling departmental atmosphere to fly to the RDF

---

2   Ismay, Hastings, *The Memoirs of General Lord Ismay* (Heinemann 1960), Chapter XIV, p.173.

3   Sir Robert Alexander Watson-Watt, KCB, FRS, FRAeS (1892–1973) was a meteorologist and radar pioneer. In 1936 Watson-Watt was appointed superintendent of a new research station at Bawdsey Manor, near Felixstowe, Suffolk. Work there resulted in the design and installation of aircraft detection and tracking stations along the east and south coasts of England in time for the outbreak of WW2 in 1939. This system provided the vital advance information that helped the RAF win the Battle of Britain.

station on the Suffolk coast with the Secretary of State and Watson-Watt; there we witnessed the first live demonstration of an incoming aircraft appearing as a tiny bleep on the original radar screens.[4]

All this, however, did not produce fighters. After Winston Churchill applied much pressure in parliament, Sir Kingsley Wood was appointed in 1938 to succeed Lord Swinton as Secretary of State for Air. He at once set out to work on a change of policy.

Rather as he had done when appointed Postmaster General, he asked at once: 'What is the quickest step to take to restore public confidence?'

I answered, without hesitation, 'Get Nuffield making fighters'.

The problem here was that – either from a misunderstanding or clash of temperaments – Lord Nuffield[5] had not been brought into the Aircraft Shadow Factory scheme and, resentful of this, was likely to be difficult to persuade to come in now. Fortunately I was able to enlist the good will and support of his right-hand man, Oliver Boden, who came down to Hampshire at once to meet R J Mitchell and see something of the production lay-out of Mitchell's Spitfires at the Supermarine factories.

With Kingsley pressing for immediate action, and in a somewhat cloak-and-dagger atmosphere, I arranged to meet Boden on a lovely Sunday morning in May at Buckler's Hard near Beaulieu. Over a drink at the Master Builder's House (later so imaginatively developed into an attractive modern hotel by Lord Montagu) we planned how to inveigle Lord Nuffield into fighter construction. 'I shall describe how we met at Buckler's Hard, where Nelson's ships were built in England's need in preparation for the Battle of Trafalgar,' said Boden. 'And you must arm your minister with a blueprint of the Spitfire when he meets Nuffield. If all else fails, he will fall for that.'

4 In December 1935, the British Treasury appropriated £60,000 for a five-station system called Chain Home (CH), covering approaches to the Thames Estuary. The secretary of the Tizard Committee, Albert Percival Rowe, coined the acronym RDF as a cover for the work, meaning Range and Direction Finding.
5 William Richard Morris, 1st Viscount Nuffield GBE CH FRS (1877–1963) – founder of Morris Motors Limited.

So we arranged to meet again early in the week at Adastral House where, exactly as Boden had predicted, Kingsley Wood found Nuffield impervious to all his arts of persuasion until he produced the Spitfire blueprint. Then Nuffield's engineering and imaginative gifts came to the fore; when Boden and I were summoned to the room, it was to find Lord Nuffield flourishing the blueprint and in uninhibited language describing the Spitfires in their hundreds stinging the beggars and stinging the beggars again, until the beggars were driven flaming out of the skies of Britain.

Plans were rapidly developed to build a vast new fighter aircraft factory covering 135 acres at Castle Bromwich – the biggest in the country. In the early autumn, we flew to the Midlands for the ceremony at which the Secretary of State and the Lord Mayor of Birmingham turned the first turf, followed by a banquet in the city financed in a typically generous fashion by Lord Nuffield.

Some apprehension was voiced there by the local dignitaries lest the siting of the key factory attract the unwelcome attentions of enemy bombers to Birmingham. This led to renewed preparations to screen such vital targets by placing smoke generators around Rolls Royce, the Hurricanes and Castle Bromwich in anticipation of future German bomber attacks.

A good deal of our preoccupation at this time was with devices and expedients to minimise the scale of destruction expected to accompany heavy bombing attacks. Lurid films like *The Shape of Things to Come*[6] and Alexander Korda's *Fire over England*[7] led to imaginative visions of near-chaos. An air staff appreciation, based on the necessarily unrepresentative practical experiences of the First World War and the Spanish Civil War, was responsible *inter alia* for an examination of the practicability of dispersing

6   Sir Alexander Korda's 1936 film *Things to Come,* based on H G Wells' dystopian science-fiction novel *The Shape of Things to Come,* which opens with the outbreak of a global war in 1940.

7   Based on a novel by AEW Mason, published in 1936, Sir Alexander Korda's film was first released in 1937, and re-released in 1944. The plot is set in Elizabethan England at the time of the growing threat of the Spanish Armada. The cast includes Laurence Olivier and Vivien Leigh.

government across a wide area of southern and south-western England. There were plans to create a miniature Westminster at Malvern and in the Bath and Bristol areas, while Harrow was at one time considered as a possible location for parliament. They say that Winston Churchill exploded when this reached his ears; but in any case he consistently set his face against any comprehensive evacuation of the Metropolis and from the time that he became Prime Minister it was never seriously contemplated.

The pressure of work in the Air Ministry was aggravated by the visit to England of a high-ranking German air mission in October 1937, consisting of General der Flieger Milch[8], Generalleutnant Stumpff[9] and WW1 air ace Generalmajor Udet[10]. It was something of a puzzle as to why Hitler despatched this mission. It was friendly, informative and forthcoming and the general conclusion was that, as part of the Nazi propaganda, it was meant to convey an impression of the magnitude and seriousness of the German preparations.

Although we too were not unwilling to show the extent of our counter measures, it seemed that the best we could hope to do was to take advantage of their readiness to talk. Thanks to the Government Hospitality Fund which provided an allowance of old brandy of unprecedented dimensions, we obtained a great deal of information – particularly from Udet when he was in his mellower moods.

---

8 Generalfeldmarschall Erhard Milch (1892–1972) was a German field marshal who oversaw the development of the *Luftwaffe* as part of the rearmament of Germany following WW1, and served as founding Director of Deutsche Luft Hansa.

9 Generalleutnant Hans-Jürgen Stumpff (1889–1968), was a German general of the *Luftwaffe* during the Second World War and was one of the signatories to Germany's unconditional surrender at the end of the war.

10 Colonel General Ernst Udet (1896–1941) was the second-highest scoring German flying ace of WW1, second only to Manfred von Richthofen, his commanding officer. He joined the Nazi Party in 1933 and by 1939, was appointed Director General of Equipment for the *Luftwaffe*. When the Germans lost the Battle of Britain, Göring initially defended Udet to Hitler, but later deflected the blame onto him. Udet committed suicide on 17 November 1941.

Milch and Stumpff said in effect, 'You are taking too much trouble in the finish of your planes and too long in the training of your pilots. We are making in the mass and training in the mass and getting ahead of you accordingly.' Here, perhaps was the cloven hoof: it was reported to the Air Council which, in the full knowledge of that warning and on the advice of the Chief of the Air Staff, deliberately held to the policy of quality before quantity with results that paid off for all to see in the Battle of Britain.

At the end of the German air staff visit, Tony Muirhead[11], then Under Secretary of State for Air, invited them down to his charming country house at Hazeley in Oxfordshire. They greatly enjoyed the peaceful English weekend after the hectic round of official engagements and were profuse with their thanks. With a characteristic touch of humour, Muirhead presented each German with an Ordnance map of the district. 'This will serve as a souvenir,' he said. 'I have marked Hazeley with a red ring, and next time you come over I hope you will remember the happy time you spent in this spot.'

After the German visit the pace of rearmament revved up to three fresh schemes in 1938. It was clear from what the mission had told us – and confirmed from other sources – that they were going to outnumber us: with the *Anschluss* in Austria in the spring of 1938, there could be no slackening. In the later expansion schemes fighters were given additional importance and gained some priority over bombers.

Whether we were too late could not be judged. The effect within the Department was that everyone redoubled their personal efforts and the rate at which men were cracking was alarming. By now I was under considerable strain myself. If it had not been for the support of Sir Henry Self – whose sagacity,

---

11 Lieutenant-Colonel Anthony John Muirhead MC & Bar TD (1890–1939), Conservative Party MP for Wells in Somerset, Under-Secretary of State for Air from 1937 to 1938 and Parliamentary Under-Secretary for India and Burma from 1938 to 1939 in Neville Chamberlain's government. Muirhead committed suicide in 1939, purportedly out of fear that a leg injury would prevent him from seeing active service during WW2.

devotion and encyclopaedic versatility was beyond all praise
– and of my Private Secretary Ned Dunnett (later Sir James
Dunnett, Permanent Under-Secretary of State, Ministry of
Defence) it would have been impossible to cope with all the
stresses of those times. In 1938 Sir Arthur Street was posted
to us from the Ministry of Agriculture, where he had earned a
place in farming history as the architect of the Milk Marketing
Board; with his arrival I could be relieved to deal with pressing
air matters in Australia and New Zealand.

And so it befell that on January 20th 1939, I left London
for Australia on an official mission with Air Marshal Sir
Arthur Longmore[12] and Sir Hardman Lever[13] to investigate the
possibilities of local production by Australia and New Zealand
of their own service aircraft.

It was a grim foggy January day in London and our friends
envied us the prospect of reversing the seasons on the voyage
to the other ends of the earth. We were also bound on a
phenomenal reversal of policy in the decentralisation of aircraft
from the heart of the British Commonwealth. This gave rise to
a good deal of incredulity in Australia: they told us that it had
always been held to be axiomatic that the British wished to keep
Australian local industry to the minimum, while encouraging
them to develop their wool and natural products for exchange
against the manufactures of the home country. That thinking,
we had to explain, had long ago disappeared into the limbo
of the past. They were still incredulous: there must be a catch
somewhere. Indeed, the basic underlying consideration that
Australasia might be cut off from supplies from Britain in the
anticipated war was so staggering for them to contemplate, that
we had to use great circumspection in deciding how and to
whom it was explained.

12 Air Chief Marshal Sir Arthur Murray Longmore GCB DSO (1885–1970)
was an early naval aviator, before reaching high rank in the Royal Air Force.
He was Commander-in-Chief of the RAF's Middle East Command from
1940 to 1941.
13 Sir Samuel Hardman Lever, 1st Baronet, KCB (1869–1947), generally
known as Sir Hardman Lever, an English accountant and civil servant.

The deficiency in Britain's imaginative strategic planning has often been criticised; but here at least the event was foreseen and provided for by the Air Ministry. What might have proved an embarrassing strain upon our beleaguered resources at the time of the Battle of Britain was relieved by the energies and ingenuity of the Australians and the initiation of this mission in 1939.

The month-long journey in SS *Orontes*[14] across half the world, with the pleasant weather conditions of the southern seas, the fascination of new scenes and in the company of so shrewd an observer as Arthur Longmore, was a new chapter in my life. In those days, before the advent of air services, government representatives rarely travelled to the Antipodes. Lord Bruce at Australia House was enthusiastic in welcoming the expedition and told me that – as far as he knew – not one of the British ruling establishment had ever seen Australia. I therefore counted myself exceptionally lucky. With the hindsight of after-years, when all the weight of the responsibility of the Middle East Air Command fell on Arthur Longmore's shoulders, it is interesting to recall some of his comments when we encountered a grim contingent of black-uniformed Nazis in the ruins of Pompeii, or when he surveyed the narrow dimensions of the Suez Canal and said, 'Just the place for aerial mines'. Similarly, I recall his reaction in Aden when he discovered that the anti-aircraft defences consisted of only two old 3-inch guns.

In my own sphere I was able to have a look at some of the much discussed staging points for the Empire Air Route. In particular, the proposal to include Ceylon in the route called for delicate handling during a press conference in Colombo where we were pressed with much oriental subtlety to commit ourselves to the main airlines to Australia making a stop at the new aerodrome being constructed nearby. The long sea crossing to Western Australia made it unlikely that we would want to

14 The SS *Orontes* was a passenger ship owned by the Orient Line. The ship was built in 1929 by Vickers Armstrong Ltd at Barrow-in-Furness. It served on the England to Australia route from 1929 to 1940. During WW2, the *Orontes* was a troopship 1940-47.

plan the route via Ceylon, rather than the more convenient and traffic-attractive line through India and Malaya. Longmore made an impromptu interjection or two on defence considerations that set off a chain of other questions. To my relief, this side-tracked the more awkward civil aviation issues.

From Colombo to Freemantle was a nine day sea voyage. After the monotony of ship routine and the steadily worsening radio reports of the German crisis over the Sudeten question in Czechoslovakia, we welcomed the opportunity to stop midway off the Cocos Islands. As a traditional act of courtesy, the Orient Line dropped mail and newspapers, together with an *ex gratia* bottle of whisky in a cask, to be picked up by the islanders for their ruler, John Ross, and the half dozen Cable and Wireless employees who manned the wireless station there.

It was on these coral islands that the German cruiser *Emden* was beached in the 1914-18 war and discovered by HMAS *Sydney* while some of the German crew were ashore demolishing the cable installations.[15] Ever since then the hulk had been progressively dismantled by the natives and converted into small souvenirs for sale to the fortnightly visitors like ourselves.

The little boatmen who surrounded us peddled their wares by attaching baskets to cords which we let down from the lower decks. The problem was to find the means of payment, as the only currency in the islands consisted of bones and shells of different shapes and sizes and these were not readily obtainable from the purser. 'Offer them anything you have which is a bit of a novelty,' he advised, so we all ransacked our baggage and I remember a miscellany of intimate articles of ladies underwear going unashamedly down the lines – to the delight of the dusky belles in the small boats. By some mischance a little cuddly Dopey from my small daughter Dawn's[16] collection of Snow

---

15 SMS *Emden*, (built in 1909) was part of the German East Asia Squadron and captured or destroyed almost a dozen ships. On 9th November, 1914 the Australian light cruiser HMAS *Sydney* responded to a reported attack on the communications station on Direction Island. This resulted in the encounter with SMS *Emden* and her ultimate defeat.
16 Dawn Louise Banks, daughter of Donald and Dorothy, was born in 1932.

White and the Seven Dwarfs – then much in vogue in London – was in one of my bags; as I knew it could readily be replaced on my return, I offered this – to the evident delight of my negotiator.

'It-laire ?' he shouted. 'Yes, Yes' I nodded back, though I had my doubts whether Hitler was really like that. So Dopey was exchange for a fine bit of Cocos workmanship and remained in the middle of the Indian Ocean.

To arrive in Australia after all these first experiences of the east and the long, rather cramping conditions of ship board was very heart-warming; to that was added a cabled photograph of our daughter [see below], taken amid her toys in her nursery at Hyde Park Gardens the day before as an especially thoughtful gesture of Sir Edward Tilshaw of Cable and Wireless. It was so clearly defined that I noticed with a pang the absence of Dopey from her Seven Dwarfs. At that time of course the wonders of television had not spread as far as this and it was a novelty to the Australians to see pictures of contemporary happenings in Britain.

Sir Arthur Longmore elected to fly across the continent from Perth. Since he was wearing mufti, he was tickled to death when

FOR YOUR BIRTHDAY
With love from Dawn

his air hostess asked him if he had flown before. Upon receiving a non-committal reply, she told him he would soon get used to it and gave him an extra ration of barley sugar.

In Melbourne we stayed at the Menzies Hotel, surrounded by clanging trams. And thence we proceeded by stages to Canberra and Sydney.

Neither in Melbourne nor in Sydney could we find any large scale engineering. Although there were prospects of utilising the big motor factories at Adelaide, it turned out that these were in the main engaged in assembling, rather than in manufacturing. It would defeat the whole object of making Australia independent in her aircraft supply if the constituent parts still had to be imported.

The Broken Hill Proprietary Company – that monumental buttress of Australia's industrial wealth and vigour – unfortunately for our purpose, was mainly devoted to steel and heavy engineering products.[17] Essington Lewis[18] – its great visionary and driving force – did all he could to assist us in our quest, and showed us all their vast coal and steel complexes at Newcastle and Kembla, but no solution of the aircraft problem lay there.

There remained two possibilities: the railway organisations and workshops offered a pool of labour and experience, but could not be drawn upon unduly without weakening the essential transport services; there also existed a promising little aircraft factory at Fisherman's Bend in Melbourne. This was where a remarkable Australian, Mr Lawrence Wackett[19], had

17 Broken Hill Proprietary company was established in 1885, taking its name from the site of its first silver, lead and zinc mine in New South Wales. It merged with Billiton in 2001 to form BHP Billiton, one of the world's largest mining companies.
18 Essington Lewis (1881-1961) Managing Director of BHP. In 1935 he visited Europe where he concluded that, given the probability of another war, Australia should be more self-sufficient in aircraft production. On his return home, he lobbied the Australian Government to establish a modern aircraft industry. This led to the formation of Commonwealth Aircraft Corporation in 1936.
19 Sir Lawrence James Wackett KBE DFC AFC (1896–1982) is widely

already got as far as the experimental production of his own design of training aircraft.

We recommended, therefore, that an alliance be made of these two resources under the banner of the Commonwealth Aircraft Corporation at Fisherman's Bend. With the assistance of the Bristol Aircraft Company in England, this alliance was able to supply the ANZAC forces with Australian machines and Bristol Beaufort when the inconceivable happened and Singapore fell to the Japanese.[20]

From Sydney we continued on to New Zealand, which presented us with an even tougher nut to crack. New Zealand was mainly a pastoral country and their railway workshops were on a much smaller scale than those in Australia. The best we could hope for was to join their needs with those of Australia at Fisherman's Bend.

This, however, was a bitter disappointment to Mr Nash and the New Zealand government. In their fervour to help they had hoped to make some more tangible contribution to imperial needs in the times of impending trouble.

There was insufficient time for us to visit the South Island, but it was clear that no suitable manufacturing resources were available there. The New Zealanders were anxious that we should examine the possibilities at Auckland, so Arthur Longmore and I agreed to fly there.

It was a Sunday afternoon when we arrived at the Auckland Airfield; to our surprise, we found it crowded with cars and people. Apparently, such was the enthusiasm for flying in New Zealand that it was a common practice for families from the towns to drive out for picnics at the flying centres if there was

---

regarded as the father of the Australian aircraft industry. In 1934, he joined Tugan Aircraft, which was acquired by CAC in 1936.

20 In July 1939, the Australian government, based on the recommendation of the British air mission, established the Department of Aircraft Production. DAP produced the Bristol Beaufort in their factory at Fisherman's Bend, based on drawings, jigs and tools supplied by the Bristol Aircraft Company, with railway companies manufacturing some sub-assemblies. More than 700 Australian-built Beauforts saw service with the Royal Australian Air Force in the South West Pacific theatre during WW2.

a possibility of seeing some aircraft. News of our impending arrival had preceded us and brought the Aucklanders out in their thousands.

Arthur made a perfect landing and we were hurried off to the central tower to address the gathering. In the circumstances there was little we could say about the specific purposes of our visit; but, inspired by the zeal and enthusiasm of all around us, I reminded them of the grim events unfolding on the other side of the world and ventured to say that it well looked as if large numbers of flying enthusiasts like themselves might find serious scope in the air in the not very far distant future. Arthur Longmore added his remarks to mine in the same strain: it was moving to note the hushed attention with which they hung on our words as if we were visitors from another planet.

Auckland itself, as we feared, held no hope as a manufacturing centre. So, after a visit to the wonders of the Rotorua hot springs and geysers, Arthur flew me back to Wellington and manoeuvred a tricky approach through the mountain gap to the new airport with an aplomb that left my heart in my mouth.

In Wellington word had reached Mr Nash of our words to the Auckland crowd and he sent for me to say that he had been thinking things over: since it was becoming clear that there was little practical hope of developing aircraft manufacture in New Zealand, he wondered whether their contribution might take the form of training pilots.

Knowing of the proposals already under consideration at home for the Empire Air Training Scheme, I felt that this gesture would be assured of a warm welcome; whereupon he offered to raise at least a thousand New Zealand pilots a year.

When we revisited Australia on our way back to England and Sir Robert Menzies heard of this he said at once: 'Well, if they can offer a thousand a year, the least that Australia can do is to make it up to five thousand'. We were able to wend our way homeward with the knowledge that Fisherman's Bend would soon be bearing its part of the burden of aircraft manufacture; at the same time, the youth of Australasia would play its part in redressing the balances of the Old World in the future battles of the empyrean blue.

Europe and London were grim places to return to in 1939 with Hitler's increasing activities on the continent. And it was all the grimmer to me personally. Although I received a warm welcome back from Harold Balfour, the Under-Secretary of State for Air (later Lord Balfour of Inchrye) and the government's thanks for the success of the mission, there had been a palace revolution at the Air Ministry and I heard nothing from my old chief, Kingsley Wood; indeed, I did not see him again until after my return from Dunkirk.[21] Beyond a few questions in the House of Commons about the changes[22] and a cryptic article in *Time Magazine* referring to 'creaking strains among the big rafters' of the Air Ministry[23], public curiosity quickly settled down and I found myself in a new position as a member of the Import Duties Advisory Committee under Lord May at Shell-Mex House: the very antithesis of the hectic activities of the past years. The most vital question I can remember there was whether an import duty should be placed on rubber contraceptives, which were represented to be competing unfairly with British products through Austrian dumping.

There was one fortunate feature about the Import Duties Advisory Committee so far as I was concerned. I had often chafed to think of spending a war at a desk and had remained on the Territorial Army Reserve of Officers after finishing my command of the Kensingtons. On September 3rd 1939, war broke out. Import duties advice was abolished at a stroke by the Defence Acts and I was free to serve again.

21 While DB was in Australia, Wood had travelled to Guernsey for the official opening of the new airport. In his speech he expressed his regret that DB, as a native Guernseyman and Air Ministry official, could not be present at the ceremony due to the air mission. ('And Now Guernsey', *Flight Magazine*, 11 May 1939)
22 The questions referred to were from Major Abraham Lyons (MP Leicester East) and Sir Robert Perkins (MP Stroud). Perkins asked 'Is the right hon. Gentleman aware of the very valuable services rendered to civil aviation by Sir Donald Banks, and does he not think there ought to be some recognition of them?' – to which no response is recorded. (Hansard *House of Commons Debates* 11 May 1939 vol 347 c677)
23 See Appendix III for the article which appeared in *Time Magazine*, 19 May 1939 which sheds more light on this episode.

I rang up my old opposite number at the War Office, Sir Herbert Creedy, on the afternoon of September 4th. As I was leaving Shell Mex House in the evening, a messenger in shirt sleeves came running after me. I had been posted as AA and QMG[24] to the 50th (Northumbrian) Division and within days I was with them in khaki at Darlington.

---

24 Assistant Adjutant and Quartermaster General

50th Northumbrian Division, BEF in France,
March 1940 (Imperial War Museum)

12
ACROSS THE CHANNEL AGAIN

The 50th Division was a tough combination of units from Northumberland, Durham and Yorkshire. They held a high reputation amongst the Territorial Army Divisions for their peacetime records in attendance and musketry training and were the traditional rivals of the famous 51st Highland Division in martial affairs.

Their General, Sir G Le Q Martel, was a superb leader, full of charm, indomitable courage and resource. His questing mind sometimes led him into trouble with his military superiors, but he was always respected.[1]

His enthusiasm for the novel and unconventional made him a great expert on the use of tanks, although the parsimony of pre-war years prevented his talents from being fully used. Nevertheless, he had built himself a one-man tank at his own expense in his private garden at Camberley.

Q was now commanding an Infantry Division that was high on the list for deployment overseas. When I arrived in the north they were already preparing to move southwards.

The first stage was the Cotswolds. That lovely part of the world was new to me and new, of course, to most of the rugged northerners from Tees and Tyneside. There was some consternation when our billetting parties first traversed the district. According to the local historians, no troops had been quartered in those parts since Cromwell's time, so the prospects of large numbers of Durham miners aroused the fears of the local squirearchy.

---

1   Lieut-General Sir Giffard Le Quesne Martel KCB KBE DSO MC MI MechE (1889-1958) was a British Army Officer who served in both World Wars. Familiarly known as 'Q', he was a pioneering British military engineer and tank strategist. His father, Brigadier-General Charles Philip Martel (1861-1945) was from an old Guernsey family. In his memoir, he refers to DB as 'my old friend' (*An Outspoken Soldier* (1949), p. 287).

Lord Normanby of the Green Howards[2] was particularly useful in allaying these alarms and the troops settled in with the minimum of disturbance.

When all were safely bedded down and the requisition notices duly delivered, I received a courteously worded letter from a solicitor in Witney, diffidently drawing attention to the sections of the Act quoted in the notices. We hunted in vain in Burford and in Salisbury for a full copy of the Act, but finally ran one to earth in Oxford. In it, we discovered that, thanks to a clerical error, a large area of the Cotswolds had been requisitioned under a clause dealing with the extermination of rabbits.

His Majesty the King inspected the Division prior to its departure for France in January 1940. Don Russell, the well-known host of the Lygon Arms in Broadway, asserted that no King of England had been there since Charles I and begged us to arrange for George VI to pass through the village.

It seemed fitting that three hundred years later – at another moment of crisis in English history – the Monarch should appear again in this world-renowned spot; and so it happened that the King and Queen delighted everyone by walking down the broad village street between lines of khaki Northumbrians and cheering villagers under the immemorial Cotswold slopes.

This time we crossed the channel from Southampton. An assembly point had been set up at Lord Louis Mountbatten's estate – Broadlands in Romsey – for the purpose of controlling troops in transit and avoiding any risk of encountering concentrated bombing of the docks during embarkation. But there were no signs of the enemy at any time and we landed punctually and uneventfully at Cherbourg. This was carefully timed to the second so that – as senior officer of the Advance Guard – I should not step off the gangplank a moment before my equivalent number in the 51st Division, who was due to go ashore at the same Zero Hour at Le Havre. In this way some old scores of 1914/15 were settled and neither Division could say

---

2   Oswald Phipps, 4th Marquess of Normanby KG CBE (1912-1994) joined the Green Howards as a Lieutenant in 1939. Captured at Dunkirk in 1940, he \s a prisoner-of-war until 1943.

they were the first Territorial troops to land in France in the Second World War.

For some weeks the units concentrated in the area north of Le Mans. The weather was bitterly cold and a succession of heavy frosts and sudden thaws kept us relatively immobilised. General Martel went forward to contact the French authorities in the Lille area, and found that they showed an unexpected reluctance to hand over portions of the French sector to British troops. After much negotiation, room was found for the 51st and 48th Divisions on the Belgian frontier. Meanwhile, the 50th had to mark time near Amiens for weeks while General Georges resolved the differences of opinion between his subordinates sufficiently to allow for the proper stationing of the new increments of the British Army now arriving in France.

During this period a promising scheme of unit hostels was inaugurated in the 50th Division. The greatest enemy in this phoney phase of the war was boredom. So the Senior Chaplain, the Reverend Reggie Newcombe, a man of great devotion and farsightedness, persuaded every unit to set a building apart in each village as a hostel where men and officers could meet on equal footing to read and write and play games. In each of these buildings an upper room was reserved for the unit padre. Here he erected his little field altar: it was remarkable to see the number of rough Durhams and Novocastrians who chose to repair to these quiet sanctuaries when the day's work was done, or even before parade in the morning. The signs for these hostels were Crusaders' shields combined with the badge of the unit. The Duke of Gloucester showed his sympathy with the scheme, as well as Lord Gort – who inspected a hostel at Quevauvilliers. During this inspection the Commander-in-Chief's military instincts prompted him to look into the back yard which contained a mass of dirty rubbish.

'I thought that cleanliness came next to godliness,' he remarked drily. In future it did.

Much interest was shown throughout the British Expeditionary Force (BEF) in this welfare experiment. After I had gone to GHQ at Arras as Deputy Adjutant General, a meeting was held on May 9th with all the principal chaplains and similar authorities: this resulted in a decision to extend the scheme as the BEF expanded to its projected 55 Divisions.

However, on May 10th 1940 the Germans crossed the frontiers of Belgium and away went all the accumulating plans for the future in the twinkling of an eye.

May 1940 brought to most Britons a psychological and often practical experience that will long remain embedded in the national consciousness.

As Lord Byron wrote:

> dates ... are a sort of post-house where the Fates
> Change horses, making History change its tune.[3]

Within a short space of weeks we had lost our century-long immunity against invasion: our aerial defences, planned to face the east, had been outflanked from the south; the sea approaches to Britain were perilously threatened and we had been forced back on to our own unaided resources. But we had found our soul.

In the quiet villages around Arras the early morning of May 10th started with the sound of low-flying planes and the bombing of Doullens – where GHQ was due to transfer within a matter of days. The German intelligence undoubtedly must have known of these plans and their bombers did effective work on the new Nissen huts erected near the Citadel; but they were just a few days out in their dates.

The 'J-Day' plans which had occupied the General Staff for months were put in hand forthwith and within hours the advance guards were on their way to the River Dyle. We of rear GHQ, who remained behind, had little to do but await the unfolding of the plans and glean what information we could about developments.

For a short while all seemed to be going well. The BEF was advancing according to schedule with a negligible amount of

---

3 'Don Juan', *The Complete Works of Lord Byron*, stanza CIII.

enemy air interference, but there was anxiety about the loss of bridges at Maastricht and the discovery that the reported Belgian defence works along the Dyle line were little more than spitlocked.

We also heard (to my particular interest) that Sir Roger Keyes in Brussels was appealing desperately to the Chief of the Air Staff in London to stop the deep bombing of the Rhine territory and to give closer support to the Belgian ground forces.

On May 13th the first news came of heavy enemy pressure in the Ardennes. I remember Sir Oliver Leese remarking at the evening conference in the cellars at Arras: 'This may be the big thing. It is quite on the cards that the enemy has concentrated his main strength under the close cover that country affords.' This rapidly proved to be true. Within four days the Panzer spearhead was within a score of miles of us and rear GHQ was ordered to Boulogne.

After the hectic scenes round Arras, which had been heavily bombed, Boulogne was a great contrast, as life in 'Hitler's weather' proceeded as usual. The girls were parading in gay beach costumes, the port was crowded with a miscellany of shipping, the leave boat came in and out; while away on the horizon, basking peacefully in the sunshine, were the white cliffs of Dover.

The Imperial Hotel on the Boulogne esplanade accommodated a large part of GHQ. Here we were joined by the Duke of Gloucester, who had been lightly wounded in the head and hands near the Belgian frontier. While the Adjutant General had gone forward to main GHQ, we set about concocting an ambitious plan of defence which – for the most part – only failed to be realised by a hair's breadth of time and bad fortune. It was clear from the German progress that the main line of British communication – which ran from St Nazaire, through Cherbourg and Rouen to the north through Amiens – was in grave peril of being severed. If there was to be any possibility of BEF maintaining sustained resistance, Boulogne, Calais and Dunkirk had to be secured. The plan, therefore, envisaged the setting up of a bridgehead based on these three ports (with others on the Belgian coast if the course of operations permitted). There is a good anti-tank water-line from the mouth of the Canche near Le Touquet to Hesdin – only some twenty miles from the series of canals which intersect Flanders and which offer switch lines for defence. This bridgehead could be manned by all the forward elements of the BEF, large formations of the French Army in the north, some of the Belgian Army and reinforcements introduced through the ports. Air cover could be given from airfields in England and, although the sea approaches could be hazardous, it seemed no less impossible to ensure them than it had been at Gallipoli.

Such was the plan we set in motion. How far it was desirable or possible to achieve is for historians to decide; what its effect might have been upon the course of the war, a matter of speculation. Would it have been possible to hold that hundred mile ring like a 20th century Torres Vedras[4] against the massed fury of Hitler's concentrations? As a result, would those concentrations have been forced to relax their pressure on the French southern armies and give them time to recover their second wind? Would the political effect have stiffened the elements of resistance in France so that she would have fought on?

The important thing for us was to secure Boulogne and the right flank. All the fighting personnel in the area, including some splendid Pioneers, men returning from leave and a snipers school at Camiers, were organised and sent to guard the crossings of the River Canche; plans were made to blow the bridges across the river; a staff officer was despatched on a wild night ride to Rouen to request that the reinforcement battalions under Colonel Vickery be moved up. Since communication with GHQ was virtually impracticable, the War Office were informed and asked to send any available resources to back it up.

For a moment things seemed to move propitiously. A fully equipped French Division came into the area and agreed to collaborate, taking up a reserve position in the wooded heights near Hardelot; some 3,000 Belgian troops offered their assistance and came under British command; as the cross-channel

---

4   A reference to Wellington's victory during the Peninsular War.

telephone was suspect, the War Office indicated in cryptic terms that they were sending a brigade of the 'gentlemen who stand outside Buckingham Palace'.

The first set-back came when the staff officer returned on May 20th, after penetrating the enemy lines, with the news that the Germans had reached the Channel at Abbeville. The Rouen reinforcements had set off before dawn and then, learning that hostile motor units were moving down the Somme valley, made a detour nearer the coast. That detour cost a couple of hours' delay: when they reached Abbeville, smoke was rising from the town. German motor cyclists had reached it one hour earlier.

Those reinforcement camp battalions might have given us a breathing space on the Canche. As it was, there was nothing for it but to blow the bridges. Brigadier Cave-Brown went forward and himself, under fire from the other bank and destroyed the bridges to the east. Unfortunately he had to leave the lower crossings to an extemporised party who, mistaking their orders, blew up the railway bridge but left the road bridge intact. By the time this mistake was discovered, the enemy tanks had nosed their way through Le Touquet and were already across on the sand dunes of Étaples.

Meanwhile the Guards from England had not appeared. They were exasperatingly close at hand aboard destroyers in Dover harbour, but some hitch in obtaining ammunition for the anti-tank guns held them back and they did not arrive until later. There were rumours however, of further reinforcements from a Canadian Brigade as well as elements of the Armoured Division, whose arrival in France was overdue; these kept alive the slender hopes of being able to maintain the defence of Boulogne. But the sands were running out. It was at this desperate pass that I took the unusual step of ringing up Sir Horace Wilson, the Permanent Secretary to the Treasury, to tell him that unless the most urgent steps were taken, Boulogne and Calais were doomed. Sir Horace communicated the message immediately to the Chief of Staffs Committee which was then in session, where it produced something of a sensation.

May 22nd was a fateful day. I was out before dawn trying to glean the latest information. Along the main road to the south out of Boulogne the chaos of traffic was indescribable. Vehicles of every description: lorries, private cars, French guns and gun limbers, farm carts, barrows, bicycles, perambulators – all piled high with articles and loaded with panicky people. They surged three, four and five deep, overlapping the verges of the road – every one headed in the direction of the port. Machine guns were stuttering in the woods beyond the valley where the railway ran to Paris. Around the quay, the Pont Roulant and the Post Office, the multitude met in swirling waves with the refugees from the north and came to a standstill.

I was making my way up the cliff road by the Fort de la Crèche when an awe-inspiring sight out at sea caught my eye. A few miles away an oil tanker had been bombed or had struck a mine. Masses of the blackest smoke pillared up into a gigantic pall in the sky, while a lake of fire, seemingly spreading for miles on the water, blazed and leapt like an angry volcano. A French soldier, dishevelled and wild-eyed, came up to me and asked '*Monsieur, c'est Folkestone qui brûle?*' I said, I thought not. '*Non, non,*' he exclaimed, '*c'est toute l'Angleterre qui brûle!*' I was often to recall that scene in subsequent days of Flame Warfare.

As we were watching this spectacle – like a macabre dropcloth against which the drama of the last days of Boulogne was being enacted – a British destroyer stole into the outer harbour, followed by a small flotilla of ships. The White Ensign against the menacing clouds, the knowledge that help was on its way and, later, the unforgettable sight of the Guards – spick and span from Wellington Barracks – marching through the milling crowds on the quay with bayonets fixed, and as steady as on the Horse Guards' Parade – had a tonic effect. The crowds pulled themselves together and cheered; but grim hours were ahead, since the German advance guards were now almost into the outskirts of the town.

Rear GHQ by this time was at Wimereux, having moved there after the bombing of the Imperial Hotel on the night of May 19th. There is little doubt that the Imperial had been

144

located by the enemy agents who mingled with the crowds of refugees, for the plane responsible for the raid ignored other targets and dropped a stick of bombs aligned so that they hit a balcony projecting from the facade. There were many casualties, but despite the danger we had great difficulty in persuading the gallant Duke of Gloucester to take shelter in the cellars. It was only by dint of tact that we were able to keep him there for even a limited time.

Brigadier (later Major-General) Fox-Pitt, commander of the Guards' battalions, was taken to Wimereux and informed of the situation. He posted one of his battalions on the hills above Le Portel while the other took up position on the high ground north of the river. Hardly had this been done before they were in action and by the afternoon heavy fighting was in progress.

The Adjutant General had gone to Calais to review the position there when a feverish situation began to develop. The balloon barrage was cutting loose and drifting out to sea. Enemy howitzers started shelling the Gare Maritime and hostile forces were rapidly turning the Guards' left flank. Our HQ at the Hotel d'Angleterre in Wimereux was like a market-place. We were faced with the strangest assortment of Dutch and Belgian uniforms: Admiral d'Abrial from Dunkirk had much difficulty in satisfying us of his identity as he had no papers on him. Many enquirers were thought to be agents in disguise and the more suspicious characters were confined in the cellar to await further investigation.

In the midst of this pandemonium the General returned from Calais and ordered out every man with arms to construct and defend road blocks outside the village. An inner guard was stationed on the staircase to frustrate any attempt to rush our telephone centre; and a small squad was set to work to burn the documents. I still picture the enigmatic expression on the face of the Judge Advocate General, Lord Russell of Liverpool, as he watched the pending courts-martial going up in flames in the garden.

About nine o'clock that evening news came of three of Rommel's tanks at Wimille, less than three kilometres away. Our roadblocks were flimsy affairs and their guards armed only with rifles. So the General gave the order to shut and barricade the front door of the hotel and pull down the blinds, in the hope that the tanks might not notice us in a rapid passage through. Then, after darkness had fallen and the hubbub of refugee traffic had stilled to the occasional clatter of hoofs of stray horses through the deserted street, the electric light failed, the cross-channel phone went silent and shortly afterwards we were cut off from all communication.

The General summoned all officers to his room. A single candle was all that could be found to illuminate it, and in its eerie light he put the situation to us. Cut off from communication it was impossible to function any further; so he proposed trying to obtain a destroyer from Admiral Ramsay at Dover to enable the nucleus of Headquarters to be transferred to Dunkirk where we should be able to carry on. At one o'clock that morning we would move out quietly into Boulogne and await the response from Dover.

Like a council of war in the old romantic tradition, he put the question of agreement or disagreement to each officer in turn. Only three of us disagreed and we proposed to make for Calais in the hope of rejoining the main forces. But the die was cast and the majority backed the Boulogne proposal.

As we made our stealthy way in the fitful moonlight across the high ground between Wimereux and Boulogne, rifle fire burst out from the *Monument de la Grande Armée* where the camping ground of Napoleon's hosts was now occupied by the Germans. By a short neck we got through to the esplanade and into the deserted port.

We planned to make a temporary headquarters in the subway connecting the platforms of the *Gare Maritime*, but it was jammed with refugees. While we were casting round for alternative accommodation, a destroyer slipped into the harbour. Admiral Ramsay had not received the General's message but, feeling uneasy at lack of news, had made a signal to HMS *Verity*, on patrol in the straits, to find out what was happening.

We had destroyed all we could before leaving Wimereux: now the cars were pushed to the edge of the quay and disappeared into the waters. Then we clambered aboard the *Verity*, warps were cast off and like a ghost she slid out of Boulogne, past the monument to British aid in 1914-18, past the ship-like fort at the end of the jetty and we

> went our way with many a backward glance –
> As one who leaves a fellow soul in hell
> Knowing what tortures waited for you, France.[5]

The capacity of the destroyer was taxed to the maximum and it was impracticable to go to Dunkirk. So the course was set for Dover and the fears of the minority that we should be severed from the BEF in its extremity, were only too soon justified.

---

5   Excerpt from poem 'D-Day' by Lord Vansittart which appeared in *The Times*, 7 June 1944.

Evacuation of Dunkirk (Imperial War Museum)

13

BACK TO DUNKIRK

Britain was sleeping as we came quietly alongside the Dover quay in the early morning hours. Up in the Castle vigilant watch was being kept, but there was little in outward appearance to show that this slumbering country had even a vague consciousness of the perils which were impending across the narrow waters. A solitary policeman placidly watched our berthing – a comforting symbol of stability after the chaos of the world we had just left. At that moment someone raised the question of what to do with the suspected spies who had been brought with us from their incarceration at Wimereux: and it was decided to hand them over to the constable.

One was fat-cheeked and like Goering, the other was short and lame like Goebbels. They had been tied up for safety in the get-away and they looked very frightened when the policeman walked over to inspect them with the characteristic knee-bend of the British constabulary. I wonder what happened to them eventually.

The General went up to the castle. The destroyer emptied of troops and a small handful of us waited on the deck ready to go back to France. The hours went by and nothing happened. We landed and shaved at the Lord Warden Hotel and still there was no news. Then, at the end of the morning, we discovered that the return had been revoked. I learnt, however, that an RAF launch was going across to Dunkirk: I got aboard and crossed the straits again that afternoon.

The oil tanks of Dunkirk were on fire and provided a great black beacon of smoke across the sky. A battery of German field guns was already established on the coast to the north-east of Calais, firing on any shipping that approached it too closely. As we neared the port of Dunkirk there were a number of sunken vessels near the narrow entrance. The *Luftwaffe* was concentrating its bombing on the quays and docks while our shortage of fighter aircraft limited the amount of overhead cover the RAF was able to give. A hospital ship with a Red Cross train drawn alongside was loading up in the centre of the port, but there was no immunity for the Red Cross from the Germans and when the bombs fell, all that could be done was to shelter the stretcher cases under the train.

Colonel Whitfield, whom we had sent from Boulogne to assist the garrison, was inside the Bastion, while Brigadier Parminter was organising the Q side.[1] Brigadier Jardine, Robert Bridgeman and Lord Munster were there from G and everybody seemed to be making a good job of it, despite strained relations with the French. Colonel Herbert was up in the forward area as a representative of the Adjutant General and Colonel Hood, the ADMS (later Lt General Sir Alexander Hood) was doing admirable work organising the medical evacuation.

With extreme pressure on the limited accommodation in the Bastion, there was nowhere to function and nothing further to be done in Dunkirk; so I concluded that there was nothing for it but to join the Adjutant General again in Dover. So we hailed the friendly launch again, took a couple of French officers aboard, and made our return. It was a nerve-racking voyage because floating mines were bobbing up everywhere in the swirling tidal channel, but the German gunners seemed to have tired of their seaward target practice and we were back in Dover by dark.

After reporting to the General, I joined Admiral Ramsay in his office at the end of the chalk tunnels which run beneath Dover Castle and emerge in the cliff face, as he coolly conducted the first stages of Dynamo – the famous 'Little Ships' operation – and saw the drama of the last messages to and from the besieged rifles at Calais.

From there, after making some of the arrangements for the reception and sorting-out of the Dunkirk remnants in Southern Command, I joined Lord Gort at Nobel House in London, where BEF GHQ was disbanded.

1   Q here refers to the Quartermaster and his unit; G in the following sentence refers to General Staff.

Lord Gort's former CGS, Lt General Sir Henry Pownall, was there appointed Inspector General of the Local Defence Volunteers, newly founded by Anthony Eden, and subsequently renamed the 'Home Guard' by Winston Churchill. (In much later days the BBC famously called it 'Dad's Army'.) Pownall roped me in to assist him with organising it, and subsequently I took charge of the Hampshire and Isle of Wight Area. This was to some extent my home county, as I had a country cottage in Lymington on the shore overlooking the Solent, where it was anticipated that the enemy might attempt an assault by flying-boat and parachute in the pattern of his swoops on Holland.

We lined up all the guns available, and they were sadly few (only five guns per man in South Hampshire and two in North Hampshire at this time!). We concealed them in positions along the northern shore and prepared to fight to the last round on the mud flats which formed the equivalent of Churchill's 'fight on the beaches'.

As I travelled around the county inspecting the gallant old stalwarts who made up the Home Guard, it was only too painfully apparent that while Winston's fighting spirit existed in abundance, there was a lamentable lack of weapons and the means to fight.

*A flame barrage demonstration on the sea
at Studland Bay, Dorset, 1 February 1941
(Imperial War Museum)*

14

PETROLEUM WARFARE : DRAKE'S DRUM

I was at a lunch party with Lord Mottistone, the Lord Lieutenant of Hampshire, at the old South-Western Hotel in Southampton on July 5th when I had a telephone summons from Sir Horace Wilson: he wanted me to see Geoffrey Lloyd, the Secretary for Petroleum, on an urgent and important matter.

So I hastened to London and found Geoffrey Lloyd at his office at Millbank. He was eager for me to take charge of arrangements which he and Lord Hankey had conceived together to utilise the large stocks of petroleum which had accumulated in Britain during the phoney war. In the advent of invasion they faced having to deny its use to the enemy through large-scale destruction. Might it be practicable to swamp him in seas of fire at the same time?

We were desperately short of anti-tank weapons. Poland and France had shown the panic that enters men's hearts when confronting tanks empty-handed. Arming ourselves with Molotov cocktails on a truly gigantic scale should be doubly profitable – not only in destroying tanks, but also as a morale-raiser.

As he paced his Thames-side room, describing and amplifying this imaginative theme, the memory of Korda's film came back to me – *Drake's fire-ships against the Spanish Armada – Fire over England*!

Geoffrey Lloyd pounced on this: 'Flame all across Britain,' he said, 'ringing the coasts, spurting from the hedges and burning the invaders back into the sea.'

Fresh from the experiences round Boulogne and with the deficiencies of the Home Guard very much in mind, I could not fail to be attracted by the possibilities of this fiery vision; but I was reluctant to abandon my Hampshire legions. It was

153

only after consulting Lord Mottistone and my military friends there that I agreed to this special assignment and took over the formation of the Petroleum Warfare Department under the *ægis* of Geoffrey Lloyd and the benevolent eye of Lord Hankey.

It started in three small rooms on the Embankment, with a typist, an accountant and no more than half a dozen others. At no time, I believe – apart from the research stations, and attached naval, military and air force units – did we exceed a hundred people. After my pre-war experience with large-scale establishments, I found it interesting to see how a small team of people could confound Parkinson's Law.

It was in the course of re-reading Gibbon's *Decline and Fall of the Roman Empire* that Hankey came across the allusions to the Greek Fire of Byzantium to which the deliverance of Constantinople in two sieges was chiefly ascribed. According to Gibbon:

> The principal ingredient of the Greek fire was *naphtha* or liquid bitumen, a light, tenacious and inflammable oil, which springs from the earth, and catches fire as soon as it comes in contact with the air. The *naphtha* was mingled, I know not by what methods or in what proportions, with sulphur and with the pitch that is extracted from evergreen fire. From this mixture, which produced a thick smoke and a loud explosion, proceeded a fierce and obstinate flame, which not only rose in perpendicular ascent, but likewise burnt with equal vehemence in descent or lateral progress; instead of being extinguished, it was nourished and quickened by the element of water; and sand, urine or vinegar were the only remedies that could damp the fury of this powerful agent, which was ... employed with equal effect, by sea and land, in battles or in sieges. It was either poured from the rampart in large boilers, or launched in red-hot balls of stone and iron, or darted in arrows and javelins ... sometimes it was deposited in fire-ships ... and was most commonly blown through long tubes of copper, which were planted on the prow of

a galley, and fancifully shaped into the mouths of savage monsters, that seemed to vomit a stream of liquid and consuming fire.

More than once in the history of the Petroleum Warfare Department attempts were made to unravel this classical mystery. Although phosphorous ignites spontaneously and magnesium, once ignited, cannot be extinguished in water, the spontaneous ignition of Greek Fire is no property of petroleum: the secret of the old recipe of Kallinikos of Heliopolis[2] still evades the modern investigator.

There were various possible applications, such as flooding the roads and the beaches with flame, fire-ships and – closer to the Byzantine model – actual flamethrowers. The first experiments – called 'Static Flame-Traps' – were very simple and were designed for installation in defiles, primarily where roads debouched from likely landing places.

They usually took the form of lining a sunken road with perforated pipes connected to a tank of petrol hidden on the top of the cutting. The flow of petrol was initiated from an observation post in which a forlorn hope Home Guard awaited his prey. The force of gravity provided sufficient pressure to project the jets of petrol all over the armoured vehicle; the whole thing then burst into an inferno when the faithful guardian threw his Molotov cocktail.

Some refinements were later introduced in the way of remote control from more distant observation posts so that the Guard stood less chance of immolation. Much ingenuity was shown in camouflaging the pipes. Across the stone bridge at Kingsbridge, Devon, the sprays were made to emerge from the gutters, in other cases they looked like handrails; but in many instances, as in the approach to Launceston or the deep cutting into Fowey, the pipes ran along the rails so innocuously that many people must have passed by without guessing their purpose.

---

2   A Byzantine Greek architect and chemist, credited with inventing liquid fire in the 7th century AD.

In all, some 200 of these contraptions were installed, mainly by the efforts of employees of the oil companies, who magnanimously put these services at the government's disposal. These volunteers, who also helped in the installation of the Fougasses and later in other signal ways, did valuable service and won to a remarkable degree the confidence and approbation of the military authorities. Field Marshal Montgomery was so impressed with his representative when he was at South Eastern Command that he created him a major (from nothing!) on the spot. Another one – Mr EWR Hardiman – was appointed after the war to the board of Esso.

A particularly useful device, called the 'Flame Fougasse' was due to the ingenuity of Colonel Livens, the inventor of the Livens Projector in the First World War. He demonstrated the effect of burying a forty gallon drum with one end exposed and a propellant charge behind the buried end, which could then shoot out an impressive tongue of flame some thirty yards long. After extensive experiments with the petrol contents and explosives, it proved a valuable supplement to the armoury of the Home Guards.

This weapon was designed to be sited at a spot where an enemy tank would naturally slow down, such as at a corner or a road block. Four barrels were connected in series as a battery, two of them filled with highly liquid content and two filled with a heavier liquid content that would stick on the tank and burn for some time.

The barrels were dug well into the bank and concealed by net in front. To avoid endangering children and animals, the explosive was kept in the custody of the local Home Guards and only inserted into drain pipes at the back when invasion was notified by the tocsin of the bells.

Hankey, with his acute and observant eye, saw possibilities in the numerous tar barrels used for road repair which normally lie along the roadside. He argued that it was only necessary to render a few of these 'live' to slow down enemy progress on the main roads, as, once bitten, the advance guards would be shy of such suspicious objects. This was done, and they received the name of 'Demi-gasses'.

Mobile companies of chemical warfare troops in Hampshire – standing by in case the Germans resorted to poison gas – were equipped with Fougasse batteries which, with practice, they could install in ten minutes after reaching a position. However, for the most part, the static Fougasses were manned by Home Guards: a total of 50,000 were issued and batteries installed in 7,000 sites, mainly in Southern England. In Scotland, where General Thorne[3] was an enthusiast for flame defence, over 2,000 sites were equipped.

The first experiments with flame barriers on the beaches showed that large quantities of oil were needed. On the shore of the Solent near Titchfield, ten Scammell tanker wagons pumped petroleum into the sea at the rate of twelve tons an hour from the top of a thirty foot cliff. Admiralty flares were used for ignition and within seconds a wall of flame of such intensity raged up from the sea surface that it was impossible to remain on the cliff edge and the sea itself began to boil.

It was a glorious calm August day and the smoke billowed up thousands of feet into the blue sky when enemy raiders overhead were reported from Portsmouth. Concealment was out of the question so the show went on. The next day a German communiqué stated that south coast towns had been attacked with excellent results and very large scale fires were observed in the vicinity of Portsmouth.

The trouble about the Solent experiment was that it was such a fine summer's day. The sea was sheltered and the water warm. When we came to try the barrage out in December on the open coast at Studland Bay in Dorset – with Field Marshals Alexander and Montgomery there to see it – the climatic conditions were very different. Alex was without his coat and, between walking briskly up and down to keep warm confided in me that he

---

3   Sir Andrew Thorne (1885-1970) was a British General with a distinguished military career in both World Wars. In 1941 he was appointed GOC Scottish Command.

thought he was getting too old for active command. Monty also was blue, with little of his proverbial 'binge'. The brisk on-shore wind, though not strong enough to prevent a landing, was whipping the sea into surf which broke up the formidable qualities of the complete barrage.

Alexander was both sympathetic and practical. He advised fixing the emission points immediately above the high water line where they would be immune from the vagaries of the weather, and this proved to be the solution.

In March, not content with an ordinary demonstration, Alexander asked to see it at dawn when he could judge the conditions in which an invasion assault might be expected.

The first light-up was in darkness and the illumination in a world of blackouts was staggering. Ten miles away in the streets of Bournemouth the air-raid wardens told us that they could read a newspaper. The Commander-in-Chief was satisfied that, whatever else was the result, the instantaneous transformation from darkness to brighter than daylight could reverse conditions drastically in favour of the defence.

Eventually the whole of the Studland coast was equipped and similar installations put in at Deal, St Margarets Bay, Rye and at Shakespeare's Cliff near Dover. Stretches were also installed in South Wales when there was a threat of airborne attack through Ireland, as well as along some vulnerable beaches in Devon and Cornwall.

Closely allied with the flame barrage was the idea of filling anti-tank ditches with flaming oil. When Winston Churchill visited Shoeburyness to see a selection of many kinds of extemporised weapons, he was shown the Fougasse and a flaming ditch. When he came to the Fougasse, his mind was too much occupied with the first prototype of the Sten gun which he had just been trying out himself in a shooting match with Sir John Dill, for him to do more than grunt when it exploded. The grunt was followed by others of disapproval when on asking he discovered that the first order for 3,000 Sten guns which he had approved ten minutes earlier had not yet been transmitted to London. 'Have you no telephone at Shoeburyness?' he asked.

But when the flaming ditch was lit he gave a grim smile as he moved back, mopping his brow, out of range of the blazing heat. I asked him what he thought of it and he replied: 'If I were the enemy and I encountered that – I should telephone back for instructions.'

These flame devices and a number of others, installed in 1941 at selected points across all the counties bordering the channel and in parts of East Anglia, amounted to an appreciable increase in the resources of the trained and untrained defenders; although, perhaps, they could have done little more than delay action while the mobile reserves were concentrated against the footholds gained by the invaders.

However, they gave a real boost in morale to those erstwhile empty-handed local forces while the surviving Dunkirk units were being reorganised and re-equipped.

Maybe their greatest contribution was in building up the great propaganda story of the Flame Defences of Britain which swept the Continent of Europe in the spring of 1941. Realising that there was no concealment for the flames and volumes of smoke of these experimental activities, Winston Churchill gave instructions that they should be used to encourage fears of unknown weapons; he also encouraged the propagandists to spread the story of terrors in store by circulating rumours through neutral channels and by dropping millions of leaflets on enemy-occupied territory.

One such leaflet entitled *Wir Fahren Gegen Engelland* asked in German, French and Dutch in the style of a tourist's *vade-mecum*:

    (a)   Do you think we shall ever get to England?

    (b)   Do you think we shall ever get
             back from England?

    (c)   Why is the Fuehrer not coming with us?

    (d)   What is the charge for swimming lessons?

    (e)   Is our boat capsizing – sinking
             – burning – blowing up?

    (f)   Where is our fleet – our air force?

    (g)   What is that strong smell of petroleum?

British Anti-Invasion Propaganda Leaflet (Imperial War Museum)

(h)　What is setting the sea on fire?
(i)　Does not the Captain burn beautifully?
(j)　Karl – Willi – Fritz – Abraham – is incinerated?
　　– drowned? – sliced up by the propellors?
(k)　When is the next invasion due to take place?

It is difficult to assess the military results of all this. There was well authenticated information of large orders for asbestos suits placed by the Germans with a Paris manufacturer. Furthermore, embarkation exercises on the Loire and the west coast of France with troop trials against burning oil resulted in more than one serious accident that filled the local hospitals.

Whatever the truth may be, the fact remains that the legend of disaster by flame in the Channel attained the dimensions of the 'Russians in England' rumour of the First War, and no doubt assisted in weakening the will to attack at the time when Hitler was hesitating to launch Operation *Sea Lion*.[4]

Another still more imponderable factor was perchance the legendary Drake's Drum which was heard over the Channel during the final phases of the Battle of Britain. I was in the garden of my cottage on the Solent one evening in the middle of September when I heard an unusual sound of reverberations from over the water in the direction of the Needles. At first I thought it was distant gun-fire, but as it continued it seemed to have a rhythm that resembled a drum beating. Fancifully, perhaps, it seemed to contain an element of defiance – although this may be due to my later imagining.

In any case, it was a strange enough phenomenon for me to remember. Next day, when some officers of the Northumberland Fusiliers who were stationed in the locality came in for cocktails, I asked if any of them had heard the gunfire. One of them, Major Robson, replied at once that they had but that it wasn't guns – it was a drum signalling, they thought, and they had been trying to track it down but could not find it.

4　Nazi Germany's code name for the planned invasion of Britain in September, 1940.

Then the legend of Drake's Drum came to mind:-

Take my drum to England, hang it by the shore,
Strike it when your powder's running low,
If the Dons sight Devon, I'll quit the port of Heaven
And drum them up the Channel as we
drummed them long ago.[5]

I asked Robson to record his experience in writing, which he did the next day. When I was next in London I gave it to Isaac Foot, the famous Lord Mayor of Plymouth, at the Reform Club[6] and asked him if they had heard the beating in the West Country. He confirmed that it had been heard there about the same time, which we checked up to correspond with the climactic last phases of Goering's bomber assaults in the Battle of Britain.

The drum is heard at great moments in the history of liberty, he told me. It was heard when the *Mayflower* sailed out from Plymouth Sound. Wellington heard it when he left from Plymouth for the Peninsular War. It beat again when HMS *Bellerophon* anchored there with Napoleon as a prisoner after Waterloo;[7] again when the German fleet surrendered in the Firth of Forth at the end of the 1914-18 war and when the little ships sailed for Gravelines Roads at the time of Dunkirk.

On September 17, 1940 as we now know, Hitler definitely decided to postpone the invasion of Britain. Can it be that his admirals had heard Drake's Drum?

---

5   From 'Drake's Drum' a poem by Sir Henry Newbolt, first published 1897. Drake's Drum is a snare drum that Sir Francis Drake took with him on his travels, and now resides in Buckland Abbey. According to legend Drake vowed if ever England were in danger, the drum should be sounded and he would return to defend the country once more.
6   According to the Reform Club Ballot Book, Banks joined the Reform Club in 1939 and was a member until 1952. He rejoined in 1963 and remained a member until his death in 1975.
7   HMS *Bellerophon* was conveying Napoleon to his final exile in St Helena.

H.M Queen Mary, Princess Elizabeth and Princess Margaret being shown a "Wasp" by Major-General Sir Donald Banks.

15

FLAMETHROWERS & FIDO

While the challenge of devising and installing flame defences occupied most of the Petroleum Warfare Department's attention during the first year of its existence, we also felt – with that deep-rooted conviction of every Englishman – that it was vital to ensure that our island fortress would not be overcome: that we must prepare to use flame as a weapon of offense when the siege was lifted.

After the German attack on the Belgian forts at Eben Emael,[1] which reduced that monumental fortification commanding the crossing of the Meuse and the Albert Canal by the spectacular use of flame, the British Army had asked for tanks to be fitted with flamethrowers. As a result, research was ongoing at the Ministry of Supply designed to meet this requirement. At the same time, Geoffrey Lloyd was also pressing for mobile flame-carriers. This led to a somewhat irregular competition between the two rival principles: of pressure vessels (espoused by the Petroleum War Department) and of cordite-operation favoured by the Ministry of Supply. This undoubtedly led to a good deal of duplicated effort, which I was anxious to cut out. So I appealed to the CIGS for a judgement, and Brookie in his wisdom appointed a day when he would himself come and see the rivals in action.[2]

On the one side were the experts from the Ministry with a long tradition of professional experience, backed by an old-established Research Station of some 900 personnel. On the other were the shoe-string expedients we had rapidly extemporised out of the resources of the Anglo-Iranian Oil Company and Lagondas at Staines.

---

1   May 10, 1940. This crucial battle was part of the German invasion of the Low Countries and France.

2   CIGS – Chief of the Imperial General Staff, the professional head of the British Army. Field Marshal Sir Alan Francis Brooke ('Brookie' – later 1st Viscount Alanbrooke) (1883-1963) held this position 1941–46.

One reads of the tensions in the training stables of fancied horses before a great race: something of the same atmosphere prevailed on both sides before the appointed day when these rival flame-snorting steeds met at the jousting place near Camberley before a galactic audience of staff officers – from the CIGS down. There were tense moments when our Valentine tank broke a vital part just before the display but, somewhat to my surprise, the pressure-actuated 'Crocodile' showed itself superior to the cordite system in almost every way – but particularly in range and duration of flame.[3]

In a sense, this was an embarrassment as it added to the demands upon our scanty resources. But Sir Andrew Duncan, the Minister of Supply, decided forthwith that their Research Station should be transferred to our department in order to complete the development which we had initiated.

This Solomonic decision of mutually-shared parentage worked admirably, so that at D-Day in 1945, a complete regiment of Crocodile flamethrowers was landed in Normandy and struck terror into the German forces. The Crocodiles and the Wasps (their smaller brethren in armoured Bren-carriers) played a continuous part in the advances through France and Germany, and later with General Alexander in northern Italy. They earned the reputation of saving many infantry lives as the Germans would not face them and it was *Hände Hoch* ['hands up'] directly they advanced.

Monty told how he saw some of his infantry go over and pat them saying 'Good old Crocs' as they moved forward into action.

During the busy year of 1942 a crisis arose in the non-stop programme of bombing Germany after Arthur Harris[4] had

---

3   Brooke's diaries record that on 27 March 1942: 'I went to Aldershot to watch a demonstration of flamethrowers. Interesting but not very promising except the Churchill (tank) fit up.' (*Field Marshal Lord Alanbrooke, War Diaries 1939-45*, London, 2001)
4   Marshal of the RAF, commonly known as 'Bomber' Harris because of his preference for area bombing over precision targeting.

warned the German people in a memorable broadcast that raids would be carried out relentlessly, day and night, rain, snow or fog. This led to a sequence of heavy losses by the Royal Air Force bombers over their own fog-bound airfields as they returned from bombing missions.

Winston was much perturbed and determined to find a solution which would beat the fogs, but the Air Ministry and Ministry of Aircraft Production to whom he appealed had none to offer. Lord Cherwell (the 'Prof')[5], his scientific adviser, recollected some early investigations in which he had participated in 1921. Knowing the unorthodox way in which the Petroleum Warfare Dept had tackled the problems of flame, he suggested to the Prime Minister that we should be consulted.

As a result, in the latter part of 1942, I received via Geoffrey Lloyd one of those Olympian documents which were wont to issue from Downing Street:-

> It is of great importance to find a means to dissipate fog at aerodromes so that aircraft can land safely. Let full experiments to this end be put in hand by the Petroleum Warfare Department with all expedition. They should be given every support.
>
> WSC
> 26/9/1942

Thus Fido was born. He derived his name from the initial letters of Fog Dispersal Investigation Operation, reshuffled by Lyn Urwick and later readjusted in the RAF jargon to Fog Intense Disposal Of.

To most of us in the Department, Fido was a completely unpedigreed mongrel. Geoffrey Lloyd, with a well-stocked mind of scientific lore from his Cambridge days, knew something of the mysteries of dew-point and the differences between advection

---

5   Frederick Alexander Lindemann, 1st Viscount Cherwell (1866-1957), a British physicist, was a close friend of Churchill, as well as an influential scientific adviser.

and radiation fogs. But to me, with little more knowledge than what I had gathered in my boyhood from the sea fogs around the Channel Islands, where shipwreck in foggy weather was almost a schoolboy collector's piece, this was unknown country. I set about at once to read it up in the *Encyclopædia Britannica* in the Library of the Reform Club and in any other works I could get hold of.

The 'Prof' put us in touch with scientists who had worked on the subject and I contacted the Meteorological Office and the Royal Aircraft Establishment at Farnborough, as well as the National Defence Research Council in America.

A conference of big industrial concerns such as ICI, the Gas Light and Coke Company and GEC was convened. Help also came from the Railways, who had worked from long before the war to get rid of fog in their marshalling yards. So far no one had succeeded in finding the solution.

Two American scientists had done some work in New England with moisture-absorbing powder and liquids to dry up the fog droplets, but in war conditions on airfields this created almost as many problems as it would solve. Another idea to filter out the water by erecting butter-muslin curtains up-wind of the airstrips was similarly unhelpful. GEC explored the possibilities of precipitation by electrical discharge, as well as a variant scheme that would shoot electrically-charged sand into the air. A further idea was to shake the droplets together by means of sound or supersonic vibrations: this was once tried out in northern California by concentrating an array of air-raid sirens as great as all the alarms in London. It made an almighty noise but resulted in little noticeable fog clearance.

In fact, out of all these ideas, the only real promise was found in the experiments in heating up the atmosphere carried out under Professor Lindemann's *ægis* at Farnborough in 1921.

Heating was very much our speciality in our Flame Defence work, so we set about seeing what could be done in that direction.

When I visited Air Marshal Sir Arthur Harris in his heavily concealed Bomber Headquarters in the Chilterns, he set his requirement for clearing a runway at 1,000 yards long, with a width of 150 yards and a height of 100 feet. Although he hoped that radio aids would bring his airmen safely into this area, he explained that, even if this method was perfectly satisfactory (which at that time it was not), the task of training large numbers of comparatively inexperienced pilots to use the radio was impracticable. He wanted to be sure that the pilot was able to see the ground when he swung in over the runway and made a decision to touch down.

Clearing a runway a thousand yards long was rather a tall order, but thanks to the upward rise of heated air, it seemed possible to meet the requirements of 100 feet. The fifty yard margin on either side of the normal 150 feet of concreted runway provided a reasonable margin of safety in case a plane swung off the runway and risked bringing the wing tips into the area of flame.

One of the big handicaps was to find a fog where we could experiment. The London, Midland and Scottish Railway had once waited two years for suitable conditions at one of their yards which normally suffered a high percentage of winter fogs; but we could not afford to miss a season in this way.

A study of the incidence of fog with the RAC and the AA showed that the Thames Valley was one of the areas of greatest frequency, so we set up a pilot installation within the vast amphitheatre of a newly excavated reservoir at Staines.[6] Other sites were prepared in different parts of the country and a mobile unit of Royal Engineers equipped with pipes and pumps and petrol tankers waited at our Moody Down Experimental Station, north of Winchester, ready to move at short notice to an area where fog was reported.

When the meteorological authorities predicted the probability of fog, I would stand by in London ready to proceed as soon as I received a call from either the station or the AA, who

6   The King George VI Reservoir in England lies to the south of Stanwellmoor between Staines and Heathrow Airport. It was completed in 1939 but was left empty due to the outbreak of WW2. It was formally opened in November 1947 and named after the reigning monarch King George VI. It is now owned by Thames Water.

had all their scouts warned accordingly. Finally, on November 3, 1942, came the long awaited chance. With my faithful driver, Jim Robinson, who had gone through many other unusual experiences with me at Arras and Boulogne, we set off at anything but a prudent speed to join the mobile unit at Moody Down. On arrival there a fairly thick fog had already developed. By the time Geoffrey Lloyd and Sir Simon Marks (later Lord Marks of Marks and Spencer fame) joined us, we had set out the oil pipes and put an eighty-foot escape ladder (provided by the Southampton Fire Service) in the middle of them.

A Southampton fireman, complete with helmet, climbed the escape ladder and disappeared into the mists rather like the boy in the Indian fakir's rope trick. As soon as the burners were going he came into view at the top of the ladder. Incredulous, we had the burners turned down and the fog closed round and blotted him out. Then they were turned up again, and again he appeared.

There was no more question – beyond a doubt we had cleared fog. Geoffrey Lloyd almost whooped for joy and Simon Marks in his quiet way was equally jubilant.

In the Sappers' Mess afterwards where we celebrated the event in strong cordial, the Commandant, Major Monkton Milnes, wrote out a little notice for the station noticeboard:-

> Got any rivers they say are uncrossable?
> Got any mountains you can't tunnel through?
> We specialise in the wholly impossible,
> Doing the things that no one can do.[7]

Within little more than a month of receiving the Olympian command we had found the answer. It was now a question of applying it. Primarily, the problem was the avoidance of smoke. It was obviously no use clearing fog if the method created so much smoke that this, in turn, presented a hazard. During the

7   Excerpt from *At Your Service: The Panama Gang* by Berton Braley, 1912 – these words were incorporated into a hymn composed by Pastor Oscar Eliason in 1942 (wordwidehymns.com).

following months our engineers devoted themselves to testing a variety of expedients for reducing smoke and producing clear burning.

When we returned to Staines from Moody Down on that memorable early morning in November, we found that the elongated braziers filled with coke had been similarly successful. Apart from an initial smoky period while the braziers were lit, this method promised a cleaner clearance. As a result, one installation was made on Lakenheath Airfield. However, the labour of handling some thirty-five tons of coke for each burning, together with the greater obstructions on the field, ultimately ruled out this method. Meanwhile, the process of burning petrol through vaporising burners was improved step by step, although it never managed to eliminate the smoke completely.

The first of these petrol installations to go into operation was at Graveley in Hertfordshire in July 1943. Geoffrey Lloyd minuted the Prime Minister accordingly:-

Prime Minister,

There is great news of fog dispersal from Graveley Airfield.

For four months we have been waiting to carry out tests with our fog dispersal installation there.

At last in the early morning of 17th July a thick fog developed. It was 300-400 feet in depth and visibility was 200 yards and under. At 5 am the fog dispersal apparatus was turned on and within seven minutes an area over 1,500 yards long and some 200 yards wide was completely cleared of fog. The clearance also pierced right up through the fog layer; the sky was seen from the ground and the runway was seen from the air. Aircraft landed successfully at 5:26, 5:40 and 5:55 am.

Then the apparatus was turned down and fog slowly gathered again over the runway. Once more visibility became 200 yards.

The fog dispersal apparatus was turned on again at

6:45 am The fog cleared again almost instantaneously and the aircraft came in a fourth time at 6:55 am.

The pilot reported that he had no difficulty in landing, the visibility from end to end of the runway, where it was lined by the burners, being perfect.

Thus we have succeeded, on this first occasion in history, in finding means to dissipate fog so that aircraft can land safely in accordance with your urgent minute of 26th September, 1942. There were many doubters at the time. The event shows that Lord Cherwell was absolutely right to press the case.

GL, 19 July 1943

To which Mr Churchill replied:-

You have pursued this matter in a most energetic way and I am glad that your efforts are being rewarded by such promising results.

WSC, 26 July 1943

Progress was steady from this time onwards and fog-safe airfields were equipped in all the bomber areas. In particular, Bert [Sir Arthur] Harris asked me to fit out the three enormous rescue stations at Woodbridge, Manston and Carnaby in Yorkshire. Every possible aid to assist the lame duck with wings shot through or engines faltering – often with dead or dying men aboard – was provided in these gigantic air havens. Although it involved a colossal throughput of 200,0000 gallons of petrol an hour to clear runways of double the dimensions of an ordinary bomber airfield, the apparatus proved capable of dispersing fog over large areas such as these: records show that in these rescue stations nearly 400 aircraft were brought in to land safely in fog.

Harris was delighted and clearly forgave me for much of my deviation from the extreme doctrines of the Bomber school in my Air Ministry days. The Royal Air Force, too, accepted it all with gratitude and characteristic expressiveness.

In an account in the *Air Force Magazine*, the famous RAF character 'Pilot Officer Prune', was reported to have found himself completely fog-bound on the way back from Berlin via Land's End, unable to land and with not much gravy left:[8]

> Binding frantically over to R/T he was suddenly told to go to a station nearby and to follow the instructions of Flying Control.
>
> He did so – and his first thought was that he was over his target once more, his second that the whole place must have caught on fire. Actually it hadn't; it was merely fog being dispersed.
>
> Prune followed the instructions and found himself safe on the ground. He said the experience was rather like descending into Hell; he had half expected to find Mephistopheles in person standing by the blood wagon.
>
> Still he now swears by Fog Intense Disposal of. And Binder (his dog) even likes Fido.

"Binder even likes Fido"

The greatest operational contribution that fog dispersal made was probably at the time of the Rundstedt Offensive in the Ardennes in December 1944. The German Field Marshal stated on his capture next year that it was the Allied bombing of his supply lines which caused the failure of this last desperate throw. He had calculated deliberately on fog to screen him and

8   Pilot Office Prune was a fictitious cartoon character created by Bill (Raff) Hooper, who appeared in a pamphlet called Tee Emm (Short for Technical Memorandum). He got everything wrong so the manual could explain the right answer. Tee Emm was written by Anthony Armstrong of *Punch* magazine who had been seconded to the Air Ministry to make technical manuals readable.

to hamper the counterattack: his calculations were well-founded for, during that vital Christmas week, fog not only covered the Ardennes, but also spread widely across the bomber bases in England. Bomber Command relied on the Pathfinders to mark Rundstedt's main communication targets; since their airfields had been liberally equipped with fog dispersal apparatus, they were able to operate despite the fog and the Ardennes Offensive was defeated.

It was, in Harris' words: 'a revolutionary change in air war, made possible by Fido.'

According to Royal Air Force figures, 2,486 aircraft were landed with Fido's help in fog conditions during the war, and some 15,000 airmen returned to safety.

Fido was a very good dog.

Pluto Conundrum (Imperial War Museum)

16
PLUTO

Pluto was the product of the fertile brain of Lord Louis Mountbatten, Chief of Combined Operations, when faced with the problem of getting the essential motive force of an invading army ashore on beaches without exposing inflammable petrol-carrying vessels to enemy air raids. He asked if it could be piped across the Channel from bases at home and was told, as with so many of the ideas he proposed, that it was impossible.

However, Geoffrey Lloyd by that time was becoming allergic to impossibilities. After consulting with Clifford Hartley of the Anglo-Iranian Oil Company, as well as the Siemens Cable Company, he was encouraged to try using the normal submarine telegraph cable and substituting the central copper conductor with water. The water would counteract the sea and other pressures, and when the cable had been laid, it would be a simple matter to pump petroleum through and expel the water.

Combined Operations began accordingly some large scale tests across the Bristol Channel from Swansea to North Devon and achieved success in practice. Unfortunately, further progress was hampered by administrative difficulties and work had reached a virtual deadlock when it was decided to hand over direction to the Petroleum Warfare Department.

I already had control for the operation of Fido at the Experimental Stations over sections of the Royal Engineers, the Royal Canadian Engineers and the Royal Armoured Regiment, together with considerable numbers of Royal Air Force ground elements. I had also been promoted Major-General in command of this young army.[1] Now, in addition, we acquired a Company of the Royal Army Service Corps and a very ebullient young

---

1   'Lt-Col (temp Brig) Sir Donald Banks KCB DSO MC TD of the Middlesex Regiment (Territorial Army Reserve of Officers) is granted the local rank of Major-General, 15th December 1943', *Supplement to the London Gazette* issue no 36306, p.5654, 31 December 1943.

navy called 'Force Pluto' which, in due course, grew to exceed many of the present navies of member states of United Nations. No one ever proposed to make me an Admiral, but Force Pluto did pay me the compliment of piping me aboard their ships when I visited them; and I, for my part, was careful not to wear spurs at the time.

The means of supplying this submarine pipeline, as can readily be seen, followed the principle of 'many a mickle makes a muckle'. Small-bore piping could be used in the difficult cross-channel conditions caused by war and climate, whereas the larger piping with which the Americans had experience and which is now used for off-shore gas drilling was not then a practicable proposition. I remember a little rotund Texan who came to help us in large-bore trials and threw up his hands in despair when he learnt what our Channel was like.

It was clear that considerable quantities of cable would be required and the full resources of the cable-making industry, both in this country and in the USA were mobilised. When this fell short of the capacity required, an ingenious engineer, Mr HA Hammick, proposed using three inch steel pipe coiled round a gigantic drum from which it would uncoil as the drum was tugged through the water. He had observed that a strong steel pipe of that diameter could be bent into a circle of twenty-foot radius and this determined the dimensions of the drum.

Tests were made in the model tank at Portsmouth Dockyard and proved the vessels to be seaworthy. Six of these strange creations were ordered and commissioned by the Lords of the Admiralty, to be known as HMS *Conundrum* I, II, III, IV, V, & VI respectively. (CON-UN-DRUM = Cone-Ended-Drum!)

Apart from the organisation of manufacture and some tricky jointing and landing problems, the cable gave rise to comparatively few difficulties and the American supplies were shipped direct in Liberty ships, adapted in America for laying the cable as well as transporting it. When the Royal Navy took over HMS *Latimer*, the resourceful Captain Hutchings had inscribed on her bridge:

Be of good cheer, Brother Ridley, we shall light such a
candle as shall never be put out.[2]

The *Conundrums*, on the other hand, had to surmount
constant difficulties. The organisation involved in jointing
many miles of steel piping and winding it onto the drum called
for special welding and feeding apparatus. This was provided
by Stewart and Lloyds at Tilbury Docks, where gantries were
constructed to rotate the drums in the water, draw on the piping
and finally deliver them like huge cotton reels to be warped
out of the docks into the Thames. Here fresh problems arose
with towing these sea-monsters against the tide. Powerful tugs
were in such demand for the Mulberries and other invasion
purposes that Winston Churchill kept a sacrosanct list of them
in a drawer of his desk at Downing Street. We had to appeal to
'Pug' Ismay[3] to get him to release a tug that would be sufficiently
powerful to overcome the tides of the channel. Even when this
was obtained, we found that it fell short of the necessary speed of
seven knots (the more powerful the tug, the greater the impact
of its wake on the lateral surface of the tow). The problem was
only solved by a landlubber, who suggested attaching a tug to
the trunnions on either side of the drum: spaced out wide, this
formation deflected the wakes to either side of the drum and
finally enabled the strange flotilla to proceed to the Straits of
Dover – defying German curiosity as to its purpose – down to
Southampton Water to await the launching of the assault.

As Secretary for Petroleum, Geoffrey Lloyd had already
instituted a network of internal pipelines, buried to protect
them against bombing. The system ran roughly in a large
rectangle: from Liverpool and Avonmouth at the western

2 'Play the man, Master Ridley, we shall this day light such a candle, by
God's grace, in England, as I trust shall never be put out': words allegedly
spoken by Bishop Hugh Latimer to Bishop Nicholas Ridley as they were
about to be burned at the stake in October, 1555. They were known as the
Oxford Martyrs (along with Archbishop Cranmer, who was executed the
following year).
3 General Hastings Ismay (nickname 'Pug') was Churchill's chief military
assistant during WW2.

corners to Walton-on-Thames in the south-east and up through the Midlands, where lateral lines provided for the supply of fuel both to the main industrial centres and to nourish the bombing fleets at their bases in the eastern counties. All these lines were interconnected with the main national storage tanks, some of which were driven deep into subterranean caverns. Major damage by air bombardment could thus be averted.

A spur ran off this network to the neighbourhood of Southampton; from there we carried the line to the shores of the Solent and under the Solent, where experiments in landing the Pluto sections were carried out with the old-fashioned type of steam traction engines which now, appropriately enough, parade on display at the Montagu Motor Museum in Beaulieu.

At Shanklin, in the Isle of Wight, a large 620,000 gallon tank was erected in a small wood on the hill – the work being carried out entirely under an umbrella of camouflage netting an acre in extent. From there the oil was fed by gravity down forking lines to two batteries of pumps at Sandown and Shanklin, respectively.

It was part of all the plans that full insurance be provided against enemy action, not only by dispersion and concealment but by duplication, so that if one set of pumps was knocked out another could take its place.

Shanklin had been bombed earlier in the war by low-flying enemy planes which, skimming in over the water under the radar beams, had devastated the picturesque row of Victorian hotels and villas that stood under its cliffs. Amongst these ruins we built our pumphouses – simulating the contents of bathrooms on a new elevation twelve feet above the debris and wrecked dwelling-rooms and hiding our mechanisms beneath. Ashley Havinden, our camouflage expert, did a fine job, as he was subsequently able to do at Dungeness as well.

At Sandown we used an old fort dating from the Napoleonic threat of invasion. The thick casemates of the old gun emplacements provided almost perfect safety for enough pumping machinery to keep some fifteen divisions supplied with motor spirit.

Sandown and Shanklin together were given the code name Bambi, whereas the alternative site at Dungeness was Dumbo. Like its Walt Disney namesake, with stumbling gait and flopping ears it sprawled all over the place across miles of inhospitable shingle wastes. Here, we were more closely under observation and, indeed, within range at Gris Nez. As it was impossible to excavate, it was doubly important to conceal and disperse. In order to deccive the enemy, the main inland piping was dug fairly openly and made to appear to branch off to Hythe and Folkestone as a part of the general plan to simulate preparations for launching the assault across the narrows of the Channel. Then, aided by the shingle, it was carefully hidden in its last stages and brought in laterally to a series of pumping stations in the front and back rooms of little seaside villas.

Captain Ashley Havinden, with his camouflage assistants, was in his most brilliant form. Behind the unchanged facades of 'Mon Repos', 'Happy-go-Lucky', 'Sans Souci' and many others, there were massive engines hidden. The villa owners would have been much surprised had they been able to walk into their erstwhile carefree resorts.

While these land preparations went on apace through the winter and early spring of 1943-44, the first *Conundrum* was given its final laying tests in Christchurch Bay. The cable ships had arrived from the USA; as far as the Petroleum Warfare Department was concerned, everything was poised for the Grand Assault.

Among the multitudes of British, Canadian and US personnel readied in southern England, or among the people living along the coasts of England who witnessed the assembly of this mighty instrument of liberation: who will ever forget the growing thrills as the plan began to take shape? Yet the secrecy was such that even those closely connected with the operations were unaware of the intended date.

I had gone down on June 3rd, 1944 to my cottage on the Solent to meet General Morgan, the Southern Command Army Commander, for an inspection of the Pluto stations on the Isle of Wight.

Cottage on the Solent, Lymington

Here, on the coast of Hampshire, I had run through the gamut of many of the typical British experiences of this war:– Chamberlain's fateful words over the radio at 11 am on September 3rd, 1939 : 'So now we are at war'; a snatched day's leave before departing from Southampton with the BEF; a midnight telephone message to my wife in May 1940 to say I was back safe from Dunkirk; Churchill's broadcast 'We will fight on the beaches, we will fight in the hills ... we will never surrender'; Home Guards in the night, patrolling the marshes; Air Raid Wardens and Air Raid Sirens; bombing of cottages down the lane and a rare huddle in our home-made air-raid shelter in the bushes; the glare in the sky of Southampton burning; machine-gunning by German planes of the ferry boat to Yarmouth[4]; Hitler's attack on Russia; the sweet church bells across the river ringing for Alamein; Pearl Harbour; and then the arrival of a vanguard of Americans billeted in the big house close by.[5]

---

4   On the regular car and passenger service between Lymington and the Isle of Wight.

5   This was normally occupied by a private boarding school for girls, but requisitioned for the duration by the military.

Now the house was crowded with them and the adjacent fields had been transformed into an airfield covered with Thunderbolt aircraft which roared out over our sequestered corner. An assortment of American-manned craft filled the creek where the Romans left their boats when they made haven under the Isle of Wight. The waters of the Solent were studded so thickly with warships, Liberty Ships, landing craft and every form of naval architecture that it seemed as if one could step dry-shod over to the island: I was reminded of the scene in the Little Russell in Guernsey with the Home Fleet in the year of the Diamond Jubilee. From utter isolation in the world and naught but the dauntless spirit, we were surrounded with the immensity of the resources of the hosts of liberty, worthy indeed of the invocation of Drake's Drum.

I was looking out to sea when strange shapes of LCIs (Landing Craft Infantry), flying the White Ensign and Old Glory, came cleaving up the Lymington River. And down the lane at the back of the cottage came the Commandos, the Gloucesters and South Wales Borderers to board them for the Normandy beaches. Our little household, with the neighbours opposite, were the last that some of them were to see of England. 'You lucky people', they called: 'See you again for Christmas!' 'Gor wot a life!' Then, strangest of coincidences, came a contingent of the Essex, my old fighting regiment of World War I. They boarded their landing craft and in the gathering dusk the queer hulls chugged out to sea. I had little thought that I should see again, as many times on the Somme and at Ypres, the Essex moving forward into battle.

Next day on the island I met the Army Commander with Sir Eric Speed, the Under-Secretary of State for War. He had given out that he was having a picnic lunch there 'as things were fairly quiet'. Never once during our tour or at the pumping stations was reference made to the abounding preparations which were reaching their climax around us. General Morgan was studiously careful that things should be treated as normal routine so that the word would go round that D-Day was certainly not yet, that this was just another exercise: after all, the Army Commander would not be behaving so casually if the real thing was close at hand. It was part of a great bluff that was pulled off in many ways. The first definite knowledge the Germans had of the approach of the vast Armada less than forty-eight hours later, was an excited report from one of their artillery officers at the tip of the Cherbourg peninsula.

The purpose and plan of the Pluto operation had altered with the changing dates and places of the invasion. With additional time there were opportunities to assemble more material and shipping and a large population of oil tins, known as 'jerry cans', had been manufactured to form the first reserves of fuel for the landing armies. The absence of serious hostile air activity enabled 'Force Pluto' to engage in running 'Tombola' pipes[6] across the beaches and at Port-en-Bessin to buoyed anchorages where light tanker craft coupled-on and pumped their contents ashore. The pipelines from Bambi were only phased in later after Cherbourg was captured. Some delay occurred before Cherbourg fell to the Americans when it was found that the harbour had been so thoroughly and ingeniously mined that it would be difficult to use it as intended. Eventually, it was decided to run the lines ashore at Nacqueville, a sandy bay to the west of Cherbourg, but it was not until August 10th that HMS *Latimer* set out to undertake the first lay.

This run ended disastrously, for when the *Latimer* arrived off Sandown with her escort of aircraft and patrol vessels, an inexperienced patrol commander dropped his hook in the wrong place and brought up the precious cable in a hopeless snarl.

A series of similar misfortunes delayed the completion of other lines and that of *Conundrum I* which had become so encrusted with Southampton Water barnacles that she weighed an extra ten tons; so that it was not until the end of September that oil was flowing directly into Normandy.

By this time land operations in France were developing at such a pace that the supply problems for our armies, far from their original landing bases, were assuming serious proportions.

---

6   The name given to this system of transfer from ship to shore.

The land pipeline on the Continent had been laid at a prodigious speed by the US Engineers from Cherbourg, on to the south of Paris and reaching out towards the Rhine. A spur ran to the Lower Seine crossings but the quickest way to nourish Montgomery's forces in the Low Countries was across the straits of Dover. So we switched all our Pluto efforts to Dumbo and as soon as Boulogne was cleared and the German guns at Gris Nez were silenced, Force Pluto set about weaving their lines across from Dungeness.

The first run was made on October 10th, 1944, after which *Latimer* and *Ridley* busily lit their successive candles in the form of eleven Hais cables from the coast at Dumbo onto the beach of the Esplanade at Boulogne. The *Conundrums* supplied a further six lines.

In total, some 170 million gallons of petrol were delivered to France by these Pluto lines, which for a period reached a rate of a million gallons a day.

Although the original conception of delivering immediate supplies to the landing forces was not fulfilled and the comparative impotence of the German Air Force considerably limited the vulnerability of those supplies, nevertheless, the savings in tanker shipping – so badly needed in the Middle East – was a big advantage. General Eisenhower described Pluto as 'second in daring only to the artificial harbours project.'

Return to Boulogne, April 1945

*(Right to left: Vice-Admiral Palliser, Coxswain,
Rt Hon Geoffrey Lloyd, Major-General Banks,
Clifford Hartley, Skipper)*

17

BACK TO BOULOGNE

Geoffrey Lloyd, the Fourth Sea Lord (Vice-Admiral Palliser) and I paid a visit to Boulogne early in 1945 during a *Conundrum* operation.

At the harbour entrance, where one of our destroyers had fought a private gun duel with a German tank in 1940, and where, in 1945, our flamethrowers, manned by the Canadians, had exacted a vicarious revenge by subduing the ship-like fort at the end of the pier, we were met by the French naval commander, Capitaine de Frégat René Kolb-Bernard.[1]

He was, I fancy, a little baffled by protocol. What exactly was a Secretary for Petroleum? Who was I? A general? A marine engineer? An oil expert? A civil servant? How did it happen, after my earlier adventures at Boulogne, that I was now concerned with the battery of pipes emerging like a Kraken[2] from the depths of the ocean?

But a Sea Lord and an Admiral was an easier proposition. He paid us all the honours he could and took us for luncheon to the comfortable quarters at l'Espagnerie near Wimereux which he had inherited from the German Admiral commanding the enemy forces in the Narrows.

The luncheon was something of an occasion. The wine from the German admiral's cellars tasted well; but more attractive still was our hostess, the Capitaine's wife, Alice Delysia[3], wearing the

---

1   (Joseph Marie Antoine) René Kolb-Bernard (1896-1965) was an officer (*Capitaine de Frégat*) in the Free French Navy. In 1944, he married music hall singer, Alice Delysia. After the war he held a number of diplomatic posts, including French ambassador to Honduras (1951-52), Nicaragua (1951-53) and lastly as French consul to the Canary Islands, where he died in 1965.
2   A legendary sea monster in Scandinavian folklore.
3   The stage name of a French actress and singer who became a star of English musical theatre in 1913 when offered a leading role by the famous impresario C B Cochrane. During WW2 she devoted herself to touring and entertaining British and allied troops.

uniform in which she had endeared herself to the British troops in Africa and the Middle East and the British ribbons she had earned by her services.

In 1940, Rommel had made his headquarters here when his troops had all but succeeded in capturing British Rear GHQ at Wimereux. With all the memories this conjured up, we toasted together the return to France.

Afterwards, they took me to the clifftop near Fort de la Crèche where, together with the wild-eyed French soldier, I had witnessed the fiery vision of the burning tanker flaming across Britain. All was quiet here now save for the gentle throb of the pumps of the Pluto pipelines which ran alongside the road, carrying fuel supplies overland to Calais and Ghent and finally delivering them direct from Merseyside to their destinations in Germany.

Two tides of battle had surged over these grass slopes: behind us stood the *Monument de la Grande Armée,* whence Napoleon had gazed at the shores of England and marched away frustrated by those faraway little ships he never saw.

Here too, one imagined, Goering stood and perhaps Hitler too, looking across at those white cliffs and watching the vapour trails of their defenders.

Her bulwarks ships, and now her ramparts wings.

The wheel had come full circle. Perhaps it was the German Admiral's wine – perhaps a deeper emotion – but my heart was filled with thankfulness and my eyes with tears, as I too gazed Across the Channel.

APPENDIX I
A LETTER HOME

*Capt TM Banks' letter to his mother on the
eve of the Battle of the Somme*

10th Essex Regt, BEF
June 28th, 1916

Darling of Darlings,

Tomorrow night we shall be commencing our ordeal of battle and the next day will see us at last over the top advance to what I hope will be a splendid and glorious victory for England and the cause of the Right. We are not down-hearted – why should we be? Doing our utmost for the highest we know, there must be an inner peace of mind which brings a contentment which unkind circumstances cannot deeply disturb.

The thought of what the next days may have in store for me does not worry me much. But what it may mean for the loved ones from which it may separate me is another thing. Heartache and sorrow and pain for many long days cannot but result. But I know, and only this can lessen the pain of the parting, that this great sorrow will be brightened by the communion of our spirits and by a love that Death will only strengthen.

O heart of hearts! May God give you the strength to bear the bitterness of the separation if it shall happen that I fall on the field. And to His grace will be added the knowledge that somewhere on the other side I shall be watching and waiting with a greater and greater love, until that happy reunion when all tears shall be wiped away.

Keep brave for the sake of dear old Blanche and Maurice and for my sake too. Surely my spirit would grieve if it felt your misery of soul. Therefore lift up your heart and look on the bright side of what is but a most glorious transition from one phase of existence to a higher and purer one – a soldier's death in a righteous cause.

God will unite us again for all eternity and love will triumph.

Don

APPENDIX II
'BANKS OF THE 10TH'
A RANKER'S APPRECIATION

The following article appeared in the Post Office Magazine in May 1934, shortly after Donald Banks had taken up his position as Director General.

On page 200, there is a portrait of our new Director General. He is the Permanent Head of the largest Department in the Civil Service, the Department which employs more than twice as many people as the rest of the Service put together. What kind of a man is Colonel Banks – what is his record – what will be his policy? – these are the questions all are asking.

His policy is known only to himself, but I can give some information that may assist in answering the other questions. Certainly, I have never sat with him on a Promotion Board, and he has never sought my advice on committee, for I am but one of the rank and file and he a departmental chief. But I have crouched by his side in a shell-shattered Somme trench; I have followed his lead against the machine-gun nests of Irles; I have tramped behind him up the Calvary way on those miles of duck-boards that led from Boesinghe to Bulow Farm; I have mended his telephone lines in evil Hangard Wood (where he was wounded but carried on until nightfall before crawling to our Aid Post in a quarry and quietly fainting away among the wounded waiting huddled in the candle-light); I have shared bully and biscuits with him in many a dug-out from the Salient to La Boisselle.

You get to know a man under conditions like these. The war years seem far away, but I can still hear his chuckle and his 'It's rather fun, isn't it!' that helped so many of us to face a particularly vile strafing with a better heart.

Colonel Banks saw active service in France from 1915 to

1918. Joining as a trooper in the Yeomanry, he eventually rose to the command of the 10th Battalion, The Essex Regiment. For a brief spell he left his beloved 10th to take command of the 8th Battalion, Royal Berkshire Regiment, but, returning to his old love, he led us forward during those wonderful weeks of the advance that ended on Armistice Day.

He won the DSO, the MC, was twice mentioned in dispatches, and was also awarded the *Croix de Guerre*, fighting alongside the Foreign Legion.

He had some narrow escapes, and in the last week of March 1918, when the few men that were still left in the 18th Division dug themselves in on the outskirts of Villers-Bretonneux and held up the enemy's frantic attempts to advance on Amiens, he was hit four times in four hours.

His most thrilling adventure, however, was on August 8th, 1918, when the 10th took part in the dawn attack on the Bray-Corbie ridge. Just before Zero Hour, a sudden fog set in, and when the parapet was scaled it was impossible to see beyond the glowing cigarette end of the next man. Down into a valley and then up the opposite slopes took us into the thick of the German barrage, and shells, smoke, fog and a blazing tank split the companies up out of all formation and isolated parties pressed forward as best they could.

Colonel Banks and eighty men threaded their way into the clinging mist another three thousand yards and reached Gressaire Wood, capturing the officer and men of two 4-gun batteries. Then the fog lifted; the little party found that the troops that should have been supporting their flanks had failed to advance. Not a soul was in sight: they were alone in the very heart of the German lines.

Counter-attacks developed and enemy machine-guns, one by one, began to dribble around. A field-gun started devilish shelling at close range over open sights. Even our own shells began dropping into the battered remnant and the cup of their distress was full indeed. It was hopeless to remain although hateful to think of retreat. But there was no alternative. Under a withering fire the Colonel and his men came back – but not all;

the lone adventurers had dwindled to fifteen. A sad ending to such an exploit.

Only three days later the Colonel had an impromptu and exciting contest with the enemy in the Bois des Tailles when he unconstitutionally assumed command of some American troops, whose officers were too inexperienced to understand the cunning war art of exploitation, and led them forward to capture another portion of the crest overlooking Bray.

The Director-Generalship of a department as large as the Post Office is a high position, but the man who is to take office is worthy of the post. On the Western Front 'Banks of the 10th' was trusted implicitly and he did not let his men down; we, too, can put our faith in him.

Sapper 3118, R.E. (Signals)
Secretary's Office[1]

---

1   With the aid of the number of online resources now available, it has been possible to identify the cryptic author of this article as Frank Heathcote Briant (1890-1973) who joined the Secretary's Office of the Post Office in 1909, and served with the Royal Engineers during WW1.

APPENDIX III
'A SUITABLE PERSON'

This article appeared in Time Magazine, 19 May 1939 shortly after it was revealed that Sir Donald Banks had been transferred from the Air Ministry to the Import Duties Advisory Committee.

Paddling swiftly and expertly along his career, efficient Civil Servant Sir Donald Banks was caught by a cross-current and swept into a stagnant backwater four months ago. There he stuck fast, but few people knew anything about it until last week. It was then announced that Sir Donald had been transferred from one of Whitehall's most important jobs as Under-Secretary for Air to a somewhat flyblown position on the Import Duties Advisory Committee.

Immediately Sir Donald's predicament had been made known, his friend Abraham Montagu Lyons began to make inquiries. At last week's end, Leicester Tory Lyons asked the Government why Sir Donald had been switched.

Answering for the Prime Minister, Chancellor Sir John Simon said: "The posts are filled by the selection of the most suitable persons." Thus he might have been explaining why the departmental manager of a business had been demoted to the position of office-boy: because the position of office-boy had to be filled by a suitable person.

Far from the centre of this minor brouhaha was Sir Donald himself, now at the other end of the world as a member of the Air Ministry Mission which is scouting out the facilities for making aeroplanes in Australia and New Zealand.

Even this errand surprised the men of the Air Ministry when it was announced last January, for the officials thought that Secretary Banks' work at his Kingsway headquarters was infinitely more valuable than the Antipodean trip.

Lowerdown officials at the Ministry did not know there were creaking strains among the big rafters above them. Sir Donald went to the Air Ministry in 1936 as Permanent Secretary at £3,000 a year, and last year took the new post of Permanent Under-Secretary of State for Air. During his three-and-a-half years of long-hour work, the RAF expanded continuously, and the consequent strain on the higher officials caused differences of opinion. Suggestion in the House's lobbies last week was that these differences of opinion had resulted in Sir Donald's transfer.

It would be very hard, however, to imagine Sir Donald making up the second of the traditional Two necessary for a Quarrel. Pleasant and quiet, he works far too hard ever to have any time left over for squabbling.

Donald Banks got into the habit of working hard when he entered the Civil Service as a second-class clerk at the end of his teens from Elizabeth College, Guernsey's leading school. In the Service, he straightaway showed his brilliant ability for organisation. Determined to qualify for high division – usually regarded as the preserve of University men – he swotted far into the night for four years and passed the necessary examination brilliantly in 1914.

When the war broke out he joined the Army in the ranks and rose to command the 10th Essex Regiment. On the way he accumulated the DSO, MC and *Croix de Guerre*.

With the arrival of peace Banks went back to the Post Office and became Private Secretary to a succession of Postmasters-General. In 1924 he was given control of the Post Office Savings Bank and introduced revolutionary changes which built it up into the world's biggest mechanised savings bank, with increased annual deposits of £30,000,000.

When Kingsley Wood became the live and enterprising PMG, he made Banks the Post Office's first Director General. Sir Donald thereupon spring-cleaned the Post Office as he had done its Savings Bank, and introduced cheaper phone calls, cheaper telegrams, swifter postal services, sweeping Air Mail facilities and the dial-TIM-for-the-time service. By the time he was finished, the Post Office wastepaper-baskets were filled with frayed red tape, and Sir Donald's only failure had been to get artists to agree on what was a beautiful postage stamp.

All this work gave Sir Kingsley Wood a mountain-high opinion of Banks, and it was Sir Kingsley who arranged for Sir Donald's transfer from the Post Office to the Air Ministry.

If Sir Donald's diversion into a backwater was something of a tragedy, at least it left the river more open to traffic. Appointed to succeed his former chief as Under-Secretary was one-year-younger Sir Arthur William Street (46), who was Banks' immediate assistant from April 1938.

Sir Arthur entered the Civil Service after serving as an Isle of Wight man with the Hampshire Regiment. He became Private Secretary first to the Agricultural Minister, then to the Admiralty's First Lord, and then went back to the Ministry of Agriculture as Second Secretary.

APPENDIX IV
SAND AND GRANITE

In Spring 1967, the Quarterly Review of the Guernsey Society published the text of their former Chairman's radio address to the occupied Channel Islands, with the following introductory comments.

In 1942 Sir Donald Banks was approached by the Home Office to see if something could be done to get over to the occupied Channel Islands a reassuring message, as it was known that despite enemy precautions, the BBC was being picked up secretly in Guernsey and Jersey. He said:

> I put the following together with assistance from the CI Refugee Committee and the Jersey Society and some official vetting. It was slanted to appear not to be addressed directly to the islands lest it arouse German suspicions of illicit listening sets. And the reference to the assurance of the utmost care to avoid harm to our own people in the air raids on the islands was suggested by the Air Ministry, as the RAF pilots undertaking these were always most carefully briefed to that effect.

> I recorded the broadcast in London and had the remarkable experience, quite unexpectedly, of walking into our living room in Lymington when I returned there [on April 24, 1942] for some of my Fido/Pluto work and hearing my own voice coming across on the 6 o'clock news.

SAND AND GRANITE

Sand to the north, granite to the south;
here, sheer cliff; there, dune of sand.[2]

So Victor Hugo described the Channel Islands and many thousands of exiled Channel Islanders remember their sandy beaches and their cliffs, and those still there, with a longing that is indescribable.

We were all close neighbours in the old days; in the town on Saturday, down at the harbour when the English boat came and went, in the market, at the Courier in Alderney or the tiny Creux harbour in Sark, we met and exchanged our news. Now Fate has scattered us. But this opportunity enables us for a moment to pass our tidings to each other in the United Kingdom.

First, about the children; very many of them, particularly from Guernsey, came over in complete schools. Most of these have retained their identity and are working very successfully under their own teachers. Victoria College is at Bedford. Elizabeth College has found a home in Derbyshire, and the Guernsey Ladies' College in North Wales. The Intermediate Schools are at Oldham and Rochdale.

Most of the elementary schools are in the country districts of Cheshire. The Vale School is distributed in nine villages there. The Castel School is combining agricultural teaching with the normal lessons.

La Chaumiere is in a large house at Knutsford. I am very glad to say that the children have kept exceedingly well on the whole, and for this, we must thank the teachers and the wonderful kindness of the hosts – English, Scottish and Welsh – with whom the children are billeted.

Now for the fighting men; the Jersey Militia have been keeping guard on English coasts; the Guernsey Militia are also

2   Victor Hugo, *L'Archipel de la Manche* (1883).

serving in a special unit; and in all the fighting services, wherever one goes, there are thousands of Islanders, as there have always been, serving their King.

The remainder of the thirty thousand Island exiles who landed in Weymouth Bay in those tragic June days nearly two years ago are settled now to varied occupations – the greater number assisting in some form in the national war effort. A great many have turned to agriculture and have been able to apply their former skill in raising tomatoes, potatoes and vegetables, to good service.

In many centres, there are Channel Island Societies helping to keep the Island ties alive. The strangeness of a strange land, of different customs and laws, is wearing off, but it's good to hear sometimes the familiar idiom and the lilt of the Island speech.

In Exeter there is a flourishing Society, at Stockport a Channel Island periodical is being published regularly; other principal centres are at Halifax, Bolton, Bristol, Bath, Glasgow, Bury, Horsforth (near Leeds), St Helen's, and Huddersfield.

In London, the Jersey Society has opened its doors to all Channel Islanders while the Channel Islands Refugee Committee focuses an immense amount of relief work and assistance, the means to do which comes from friends from all over the world.

As to the Islands themselves, there is little news beyond the occasional brief messages through the Red Cross. When we've heard occasionally of an air raid, we Islanders have felt apprehensive, but I can give the assurance that the utmost care is taken to avoid harm to our own people.

Sand and granite – out of the sand and the soil the industry of Channel Islanders has built up their past prosperity. On the rock, they founded their homes and their characters. The same steadfastness will see us through dark days to happier times.

TIMELINE

1891	Born in St Peter Port, Guernsey
1899-1909	Attended Elizabeth College, Guernsey
1909	Joined Civil Service, Exchequer & Audit Office
	Joined London Yeomanry
1914	Passed Civil Service Examination
1914	Private in London Yeomanry
1915	Jan: commissioned, temp 2nd Lieutenant
	Joined 10th Essex Regiment
	Jul: arrived in France
1916	Promoted to temp Captain
	Jul: admitted to hospital with 'Blighty wound'
1917	Jan: returned to battalion in France
	Apr: awarded MC
	Oct: promoted to temp Major
1918	Jan: attended Senior Officers' School
	Apr: rejoined battalion, appointed commanding officer, 10th Essex Regiment
	Jul: appointed acting Lieut-Colonel, 8th Royal Berks Regt
	Oct: awarded DSO
	Nov: promoted to temp Lieut-Colonel, Mentioned in dispatches
1919	Feb: awarded *Croix de Guerre*
	May: demobilised - rejoined Civil Service: General Post Office
1921	Marriage to Dorothy Webster in Woking
	Publication of *With the 10th Essex in France*
1924	Appointed Deputy Controller, Post Office Savings Bank
1927	Appointed commanding officer of Princess Louise's Kensington Regt
1931	Appointed Controller, Post Office Savings Bank
1932	Birth of daughter Dawn

1934	Appointed Director General of the Post Office
1935	Knighted in New Year's Honours List
	Led Transatlantic Air Mission
	to Ottawa and Washington
1936	Appointed Permanent Secretary
	to the Air Ministry
1939	Air Mission to Australia & New Zealand
	Appointed Director General, Import Duties
	Advisory Committee
1939	Joined 50th Northumbrian Regiment, BEF
1940	Evacuated from Boulogne
	Appointed Director General,
	Petroleum Warfare Department
1942	Broadcast *Sand and Granite* on BBC
	Awarded Efficiency Decoration (TD)
1943	Founded the Guernsey Society
	Director of Elizabeth College in exile
1944	D-Day – PLUTO
	Publication of *Nos Iles*
1945	Liberation of the Channel Islands
1946	Awarded Legion of Merit by US President
	Publication of *Flame Over Britain*
1947	Death of wife Dorothy, Hampshire
	Retirement from Civil Service
	Appointed Director of De La Rue
1948	Marriage to Elizabeth Bradley in Westminster
1949	Birth of son Peter
1951	Birth of daughter Melanie
1975	Death in New Forest, Hampshire

ABBREVIATIONS

AA	Automobile Association
ANZAC	Australia and New Zealand Army Corps
BBC	British Broadcasting Corporation
BEF	British Expeditionary Force
CGS	Chief of General Staff
CIGS	Chief of the Imperial General Staff
CO	Commanding Officer
CPR	Canadian Pacific Railroad
DB	Sir Donald Banks
DSO	Distinguished Service Order
GHQ	General Headquarters
GPO	General Post Office
GSO	General Staff Officer
HMAS	His/Her Majesty's Australian Ship
HMS	His/Her Majesty's Ship
HQ	Headquarters
IFS	Irish Free State
LCI	Landing Craft Infantry
MC	Military Cross
MP	Member of Parliament
NCO	Non-Commissioned Officer
OTC	Officer Training Corps
PMG	Postmaster General
POW	Prisoner of War
PRO	Public Relations Officer
PWD	Petroleum Warfare Department
QMG	Quarter Master General
RAC	Royal Automobile Club
RAF	Royal Air Force
RAMC	Royal Army Medical Corps
RDF	Range and Direction Finding / Radar Direction Finder
RHA	Royal Horse Artillery
SNO	Senior Naval Officer

BIBLIOGRAPHY

Books by Sir Donald Banks

Banks, Sir Donald, *Flame Over Britain* (Sampson Low, Marston & Co, 1946)

Banks, TM & RA Chell, *With the 10th Essex in France* (London, 1921)

Nos Iles: A Symposium on the Channel Islands (Channel Islands Study Group, 1944)

Other sources

Bailey, Sgt OF and Hollier, HM, *The Kensingtons 13th London Regiment* (Regimental Old Comrades Association, 1935)

Benn, Tony, *Out of the Wilderness: Diaries 1963-67* (Arrow, 1988)

Brech, Edward, Andrew Thomson & John F. Wilson, *Lyndall Urwick, Management Pioneer: A Biography* (Oxford, 2010)

Brooke, Alan, *Field Marshal Lord Alanbrooke, War Diaries 1939-45* (London, 2001)

Campbell-Smith, Duncan, *Masters of the Post: the Authorized History of the Royal Mail* (Allen Lane, 2011)

Drake-Brockman, DH, *Elizabeth College Register, Vol II, 1874-1911* (Guernsey, 1931)

Gillies, Midge, *Waiting for Hitler: Voices from Britain on the Brink of Invasion* (Hodder & Stroughton, 2006) - Chapter 15

Hay, Ian, *The First Hundred Thousand* (Blackwood, 1915)

Hayward, James, *The Bodies on the Beach: Sealion, Shingle Street and the Burning Sea Myth of 1940* (CD41 Publishing, 2001)

Hyde, H Montgomery, *British Air Policy Between the Wars, 1918-1939* (Heinemann, 1976)

Ismay, Hastings, *The Memoirs of General Lord Ismay* (Heinemann 1960)

Longmore, Sir Arthur, *From Sea to Sky, 1910-45* (Geoffrey Bles, 1946)

Martel, Sir Giffard, *An Outspoken Soldier* (Sifton Praed, 1949)

Nichols, GHF, *The 18th Division in the Great War* (Blackwood, 1922)

O'Halpin, Eunan, *Head of the Civil Service: A Study of Sir Warren Fisher* (Routledge, 1989)

Pugh, Peter, *The Highest Perfection: A History of De La Rue* (Icon Books, 2011)

Reith, John, *Into the Wind* (Hodder & Stoughton, 1949)

Searle, Adrian, *PLUTO: Pipeline Under the Ocean* (Shanklin Chine, 1995)

St Johnston, Eric, *One Policeman's Story* (Barry Rose, 1978)

INDEX

Gardiner, Sir Thomas 110, 119
Gas Light and Coke Company 168
GEC 168
Geddes, Sir Eric 113
General Post Office (GPO) v, ix, xii,
    xiii, xiv, xv, xvi, 10, 38, 65–79,
    80–8, 95, 99–117, 144, 191,
    193, 195, 196, 201, 202, 203.
    See also emergency services,
    kiosks, off-peak call rates,
    Speaking Clock, telegram
German Air Force 185.
    See also Luftwaffe
    mission to UK 124–5
Gibson, Sir Henry 15
Gilbert Scott, Sir Giles ix, 109
Gladstone, William Ewart 8, 67, 81
Gloucester, Duke of 139, 141, 145
Godfrey, David xv
Goebbels, Joseph 28, 149
Goering, Hermann 149, 162, 188
Gort, Lord 139, 150–1
Gott, Captain 'Strafer' 92–3
GPO North 66–7, 100
GPO South 68–9
Graveley Airfield 171
Greek Fire 154–5
Green Howards 138
Gressaire Wood 51–3, 192
Gris Nez 181, 185
Guernsey iii, v, ix, x, xiii, xiv, xv, xvi,
    xvii, 1, 2, 6, 7, 13, 19, 71, 133,
    137, 183, 195, 197, 198, 201,
    202, 203, 205
    Lieutenant-Governor of xv
Guernsey Society viii, xiv, xv, xvi, xvii,
    197, 202
Guildhall Library 10

H

Haig, Sir Douglas 16, 30, 39, 47, 49
Haldane, Richard 91
Hammick, H A 178
Hangard Wood 45, 47, 191
Hankey, Lord 153–6
Hansard 75, 133
Le Hardelot 37, 94, 142
Hardiman, E W R 156
Harris, Sir Arthur 'Bomber' 166, 168,
    172, 174

Hartley, Clifford 177, 186
Havinden, Capt Ashley 180–1
Le Havre 138
Hecq 60
Henley Business School 101
Herbert, Colonel 150
Hesdin 142
Hill, Rowland 67, 68, 70, 107
Hindenburg Line 39, 58–9
Hitler, Adolf 124, 129, 133, 141, 142,
    161, 162, 182, 188, 205
HM Stationery Office 84, 86–7
Home Guard 151, 153, 155
Home Office xiv, 9, 76, 197
Hood, Sir Alexander 150
House of Commons xiii, 74, 87, 133
Howe, C D 116
Howitt, John 20, 31, 35
Hudson, Colonel N B 57
Hugo, Victor 198
Hume, Sir Nutcombe 58
Hunt, Willie 20
Hurricane 123
Hyde Park 71, 72, 129
Hyderabad Barracks, Colchester 18–19
Hythe 181

I

ICI 168
Illingworth, A H 73
Imperial Airways 113
Imperial War Museum xii, xvii, 36, 136,
    148, 152, 160, 176
Import Duties Advisory Committee xiii,
    133, 194
Indian Civil Service 10, 19
Irish Free State 78, 114–15, 203
Isle of Wight 37, 151, 180–3, 196
Ismay, Lord Hastings 121, 179, 205

J

Jardine, Brigadier 150
Joynson-Hicks, Sir William 79

K

Kellaway, F G 76, 77, 78
Kensington 46, 67, 79, 80, 90–97, 201
Kensington War Memorial 94, 96